Connecting Teens with Technology at the Library

The Teen Librarian Bookshelf

About the Series

The Teen Librarian Bookshelf is designed to be a comprehensive resource for young adult librarians. The series provides the breadth and depth of information that teen librarians need to serve the teen audience in school and public libraries. With their experience and expertise, authors in the series are mentors for librarians serving tweens and teens.

About the Series Editor

RoseMary Ludt has written and edited for the young adult librarian audience for nearly twenty years, working for Neal-Schuman Publishers, Kurdyla Publishing LLC, and American Library Association. She was the editor-in-chief of *VOYA Magazine* for ten years and is a former editor for VOYA Press and *YALS Journal*. Among her books are *101+ Teen Programs That Work* and *More Teen Programs That Work*.

Before her writing and editing career, Ludt worked twenty-five years in the Coshocton Public Library. While there, she created the position of young adult services coordinator and served eleven years in the position. Some of her original programs are still enjoyed by teens at the library.

Ludt presented over seventy workshops, keynotes, and audio and video presentations for librarians serving teen and senior adults in the United States and Canada, encouraging librarians to connect with their audiences by working and creating with them.

Coming full circle, Ludt has returned to libraries, working in the circulation department of Muskingum County Library System in Ohio.

Books in the Series

Totally Tweens & Teens: Youth-Created and Youth-Led Library Programs edited by Diane P. Tuccillo
Think Big!: A Resource Manual for Teen Library Programs That Attract Large Audiences edited by Rose-Mary Ludt
Connecting Teens with Technology at the Library by Kelly Nicole Czarnecki and Marie L. Harris

Connecting Teens with Technology at the Library

Kelly Nicole Czarnecki and
Marie L. Harris

ROWMAN & LITTLEFIELD
Lanham • Boulder • New York • London

Published by Rowman & Littlefield
An imprint of The Rowman & Littlefield Publishing Group, Inc.
4501 Forbes Boulevard, Suite 200, Lanham, Maryland 20706
www.rowman.com

6 Tinworth Street, London SE11 5AL

Copyright © 2021 by The Rowman & Littlefield Publishing Group, Inc.

All rights reserved. No part of this book may be reproduced in any form or by any electronic or mechanical means, including information storage and retrieval systems, without written permission from the publisher, except by a reviewer who may quote passages in a review.

British Library Cataloguing in Publication Information Available

Library of Congress Cataloging-in-Publication Data Available

Names: Czarnecki, Kelly Nicole, 1974– author. | Harris, Marie, 1985– author.
Title: Connecting teens with technology at the library / Kelly Nicole Czarnecki and Marie L. Harris.
Description: Lanham : Rowman & Littlefield, [2021] | Series: The teen librarian bookshelf | Includes bibliographical references and index. | Summary: "Connecting Teens with Technology at the Library presents a balanced view of the often complex relationship between teenagers and their technology. The authors share more than a dozen full lesson plans for technology-based programs, scalable for any library budget, that will help the reader to engage with their teenaged patrons"—Provided by publisher.
Identifiers: LCCN 2020056366 (print) | LCCN 2020056367 (ebook) | ISBN 9781538135877 (cloth) | ISBN 9781538135884 (paperback) | ISBN 9781538135891 (ebook)
Subjects: LCSH: Libraries and teenagers—United States. | Young adults' libraries—Activity programs—United States. | Young adults' libraries—Information technology—United States.
Classification: LCC Z718.5 .C98 2021 (print) | LCC Z718.5 (ebook) | DDC 027.62/6—dc23
LC record available at https://lccn.loc.gov/2020056366
LC ebook record available at https://lccn.loc.gov/2020056367

I dedicate this book to those who want to be the change for youth today.
—Kelly Nicole Czarnecki

I dedicate this book to all of the talented and passionate youth-serving library staff I have worked with over the years. They are a continual inspiration.
—Marie L. Harris

Contents

Series Editor's Foreword	ix
Foreword	xi
Preface	xiii

Part I: Getting Started — 1
1. Technology and Today's Youth — 3
2. Technology Setup — 13
3. Funding Technology — 19
4. Aligning Technology Programs with Your Library's Mission — 27

Part II: Connecting Teens with Technology — 35
5. Mentorship — 37
6. Career Readiness and Exploration — 47
7. Partnerships and Collaboration — 55

Part III: Technology in Practice — 59
8. Tech without Tech — 61
9. Making, Makerspaces, and the Maker Movement — 69
10. Collection Development — 77
11. Sample Technology Programs — 83

Index	97
About the Authors	101

Series Editor's Foreword

Technology is more important than ever for people to communicate with one another during the era of the COVID-19 pandemic. It has become essential as a means for libraries to stay connected with teens. Young adult librarians have been on the forefront for devising ways to keep their teen audiences involved with library information and activities through programs and videos, communication venues, and more. Thankfully, there were librarians who could lead the way. Kelly Nicole Czarnecki and Marie L. Harris are two of those who have worked with technology for many years at ImaginOn, a branch of the Charlotte Mecklenburg Library that focuses on youth aged 10 to 18.

With *Connecting Teens with Technology at the Library*, Czarnecki and Harris have created an essential manual for working with teens through and with technology. From matching your program with the library's mission, to developing your professional and teen collections with technology-centered materials, to sample programs that your teens will love, this book has everything you need to create an impactful technology program that works in and out of the library.

The comprehensive Teen Librarian Bookshelf is a go-to series of books and resources for the YA librarian. This new series plans to cover the breadth and depth of current information that teen librarians need to serve the teen and tween audiences in school and public libraries by drawing on the voices of experienced experts. The authors of this series will become the teen librarian's favorite mentors.

—RoseMary Ludt, Series Editor
Teen Librarian Bookshelf

Foreword

I met Marie and Kelly when I was in high school in 2014. At the time, I was often coming to ImaginOn and would stay in their teen-designated area called the Loft. One of the most memorable programs that I attended was a lesson hosted by Marie. She taught a small group of participants how to crochet. We crocheted squares that were stitched together to create a blanket for someone less fortunate. That program was one of my favorites but was only one of many programs I would attend throughout high school. In that program, I was able to learn an actual skill, contribute to society, and do something productive. All of Marie and Kelly's programs were designed to educate, create, and invest in its participants. I know that this book will do the same for its reader because Marie and Kelly were a part of my story.

As a recipient of their service, I can attest that they not only know how to engage young adults but can connect them to essential resources for creating career connections. My first job was at ImaginOn. I was a docent at the beloved Clifford the Big Red Dog exhibit. When at the exhibit, co-workers and I would share the responsibilities of making sure children did not run out of the exhibit, brief adults on the rules, make copies, and complete other administrative tasks. I gained technical and problem-solving skills, and if I ever needed guidance I would go to the Loft and ask the staff for help. ImaginOn's staff helped me to foster the skills necessary for professional development. Included in this book are outlines for some of the engaging technology programs, including career-focused ones, which benefited me. Marie and Kelly have written this book as a resource on how to develop tech-oriented programming for various skill and funding levels. Through this book, readers are guided and informed on how to create the same successful outcomes in their facilities.

Considering the pandemic, young adults need services and programs more than ever. Right now is the time for young adult tech service supporters to further invest in their community. Combined, Marie and Kelly have spent more than two decades pouring knowledge into students and young adults like me and are going to further their impact through this book. I remember seeing Marie teaching young adults how to code for the first time, how the participants were enjoying the program, and how easy the program was to follow, like the ready-to-go programs in this book. Kelly and she both made sure that their tech-friendly programs were inclusive and cultivated an appreciation for tech while still engaging their participants in creative ways. At ImaginOn, they were a credible and readily available source for all my questions. They helped cultivate an informative and tech-friendly environment. I wanted to become a part of that community so much so that I became the first Public Library Association intern at ImaginOn through the inclusive internship initiative.

Within that internship, I was mentored for the first time. I learned what my library had to offer through shadowing and volunteering. My main project was to create book kits. I spent hours researching books, activities, and discussion questions. I chose books that had characters of various ethnicities who were relatable, complex, and faced real challenges. Marie and Kelly made sure in this book to address serving communities with different challenges, such as at-risk youth. They discuss their experiences and provide guidance for helping to embrace their differences while still being able to serve them accordingly. My project reflected what I saw in my own community. I have seen their diligent work ethic on more than one occasion.

One afternoon, I went to a session taught by Marie on how to use and create vinyl stickers. That session lasted several hours, and she was so patient with the group. If we messed up or could not get the software to respond correctly, she would redirect us to the instructions. She also told the group about how to use other equipment at the library, like the wood-engraving tool for creating business logos. She knows how to connect creativity to productivity. Along with the technical side of our library, I saw the social connections that drove the librarians. On one occasion, I went to a community center to assist with a program for senior citizens. The goal was to register them for library cards. This book expresses the impact and importance of intergenerational access to technology. The library community knows the importance of helping senior citizens. Our library branch helped with managing devices and apps. I decided after the internship to be a librarian. I saw how keeping people informed about services, resources, and programs had a direct positive impact on a community. Right after that internship, I started community college.

Near the end of my first semester, all the interns were gathered up to present their projects. I practiced in front of the library staff at ImaginOn twice. At the time, I was also taking an intro to communication class. I was trying to implement all that I had learned to represent my library and everyone from it who had supported me. I had never presented anything this significant before. I knew that this was a time to implement the skills and professionalism I gained from all the mentoring, shadowing, and volunteering. When I finished, I sent a recording of myself to my professor, and she nominated me to be a student representative of my community college. From then on, I would go to class and tell students about the resources our college had to offer. It was a sign of my personal growth, which I attribute to my supportive library community. They took the time to show me how to connect people with resources, and now I was doing it on behalf of my college. I chose to pursue the same career that had the most impact on my life.

Imagine the impact that this book will have on those who implement these career-altering additional programs into their young adult services. Young adults are experiencing a huge need for people like Marie and Kelly. They are advocating for progressive and forward-thinking individuals to respond to the need as well. As a college student, I am experiencing a huge shift of in-person resources to online resources. Like many others, personal, work, and school life is online, so we rely on technology every day. To serve young adults, it is a necessity to be able to incorporate tech or at least have it as a resource. It would be a disservice to yourself to read this book and not incorporate any of its supported knowledge. All my accomplishments have been supported or initiated by my library, and I hope that this book will be of assistance to others looking to create lasting change in the young adults they serve.

—Jeneva Claiborne

Preface

When you expect the wave, you can ride the wave.[1]

—Jessamyn Stanley

While this statement was made in the context of a podcast that was challenging stereotypes, it still applies to teens and technology in the library, especially in 2021. In other words, change is constant—particularly with technology, teens, and libraries. We need to change up some of our approaches with engaging teens. During the time this book was written, many teens have participated in remote learning or are online for schooling because of the pandemic. Many libraries are also only able to offer virtual programming, if at all. Screen time from morning until night can cause burnout, and the critical needs of teens likely have changed. Did the same approaches ever really work anyway to benefit those who might need access the most? What inequities exist; that is, who has access to the internet outside of the library and school? Who is getting suspended from school or the library more often? Who has regular access to food, affecting learning and participation? The list goes on, but can the library play a more active and instrumental role in addressing those inconsistencies? An article in *School Library Journal* says, "What has changed is that library staff is seeing these disparities more clearly in their communities every day, and there is an uncertainty of what the future holds for learning, economic advancement, and civic engagement."[2]

Fortunately, we have a lot in our corner that can help us navigate this ever-changing landscape. Start with taking direction and inspiration from teens by asking for their thoughts about what they are interested in and what they would like to see at the library for them. Teens are who we are trying to engage in our libraries and likely one reason you are reading this book. Start from a solid foundation to make decisions that can meet teens' critical needs where they are and rise to meet some of the challenges they face and may have inherited as part of their community.

Partnerships and relationship-building are at the cornerstone of our work. They will guide us in rethinking what library services with a technology focus can be for youth. They are also part of the change to which we need to adapt to stay relevant and vital.

THE PURPOSE OF THIS BOOK

Connecting Teens with Technology at the Library will help support fellow teen-serving staff nationwide in technology program creation and collection development. Technology is a continually changing field, and this book will update readers on the newest resources. In nearly every news cycle, we learn of new needs in technology-related areas, and libraries are often poised to provide teens with their first introduction to possibilities beyond high school graduation. Beyond a mere listing of program ideas or reviews of upcoming technology, there is practical advice for linking these technology programs and materials with real-world applications such as potential careers, mentorships, and community partnerships. We will also discuss the scalability of programs to fit any budget and collection development to support your technology. We believe that teen-serving library staff in public and school libraries will be eager to purchase and read this volume.

Connecting Teens with Technology at the Library presents a balanced view of the often-complicated relationship between teenagers and their technology. The authors share more than a dozen full lesson plans for technology-based programs, scalable for any library budget, helping the reader engage with their teenaged patrons. The reader will also learn how technology-based programs can help teens prepare for post–high school vocations and how to build valuable community partnerships that can help take your programs to the next level.

READERS FOR THIS BOOK

While the focus is on working with teens and libraries, both public school teachers and school staff will be interested in this book's information. Digital media spaces or after-school community connectors will also find relevancy in the work. Places such as museums and even youth group homes looking to freshen their technology offerings and approaches would be remiss in not checking out the most applicable content. Feel free to pass a copy on to someone who has asked questions about their teens and tech space.

GUIDE TO READING THIS BOOK

You are welcome to enjoy this resource from cover to cover or focus on the areas that you are most interested in and skip around throughout the book. Here is a look at what is included in each chapter.

Chapter 1, "Technology and Today's Youth," gives a broad overview of teens and technology's landscape as of this writing. It helps us keep our mindset in a place that can support teens where they are and gives us the tools to let teens lead the way to their passions and interests.

Chapter 2, "Technology Setup," is where we look at approaches to physical and virtual setups. Included are recommended starting points for facilities that are building from the ground up and those that want to refresh their spaces.

Chapter 3, "Funding Technology," gives a holistic approach to various funding models for libraries. There are options and examples of fundraising, grants, and other sources, depending on your library's structure. Get tips here on how to help make your—and the teens'—ideas into reality.

Chapter 4, "Aligning Technology Programs with Your Library's Mission," takes a look at several library systems' mission statements. It then ties this crucial guiding principle with programming, specifically that of teens and technology. If you have concerns for making a case as to why technology is essential and how it fits within equity, diversity, and inclusion measurements, this chapter is a great place to start.

Chapter 5, "Mentorship," looks at fresh definitions of the mentoring relationship. We give the perspective of advising another staff member who is either new to the profession or has specific needs around working with teens and technology in the library. We also look at creating a structure of mentoring teens at the library through technology and give an example structure that has been in the works for about fifteen years.

Chapter 6, "Career Readiness and Exploration," is a great chapter to explore how to add further structure to your existing technology career programming for teens. Tips on connecting teens with their interests that may grow beyond the library round out this useful read.

Chapter 7, "Partnerships and Collaboration," looks at some examples of working with other organizations from a technology focus. This chapter shares how to determine the community's needs and how the pandemic has changed how we work with others.

Chapter 8, "Tech without Tech," gives great ideas for low- or no-tech programs related to outreach, makerspaces, and more that involve little to no devices. Go to this section to get started, especially if you have a smaller budget, are looking for ideas outside of the box, or want to gain more experience with using technology in your programs.

Chapter 9, "Making, Makerspaces, and the Maker Movement," includes various models for your library, some concrete examples of existing spaces, as well as programming ideas. We demonstrate how to use the lens of inclusivity when designing a space. We must consider who may be left out of the conversation unintentionally through the space's design and organization and how you can improve it.

Chapter 10, "Collection Development," gives lists of recommended resources for staff and young adult reads for teens centered around technology. You will feel fortified and supported with these well-researched lists if wanting to further flesh out the technology piece for your library or organization.

Chapter 11, "Sample Technology Programs," presents exciting ideas on how to engage teens through programming with the main topics from the previous chapters.

After you have finished reading *Connecting Teens with Technology at the Library*, you may have more questions about your particular situation, but you will have the resources for the next step. You will also have more enthusiasm and motivation to get started and envision the possibilities!

NOTES

1. Saad, Layla. Audio blog. *Good Ancestor*. Layla Saad. September 24, 2020. http://laylafsaad.com/good-ancestor-podcast/ep031-jessamyn-stanley.

2. Subramaniam, Mega, and Linda W. Braun. "COVID-19 Is an Opportunity to Rethink Youth Librarianship: Reimagining Libraries." *School Library Journal*. May 31, 2020. Accessed September 29, 2020. https://www.slj.com/?detailStory=covid-19-is-an-opportunity-to-rethink-youth-librarianship-reimagining-libraries.

Part I

Getting Started

ONE
Technology and Today's Youth

My co-worker and I were talking about defining the makerspace ("Makerspaces are, simply put, places where people make things" according to Ellyssa Kroski in *The Makerspace Librarian's Sourcebook*[1]) and then the staff's responsibility. She brilliantly stated, "More and more, there's a line in the sand about what technology we're expected to know how to use, and that line always keeps moving." She is right. Technology continues to change, so what you might learn in a library school can look quite different from what you use when working in a library. It might look quite different from one college to another and even from one library branch to another within the same system. As with any profession, our library degrees gave us a solid foundation in inquiry and the ability to solve problems no matter what new gadget is presented. Yet the technology evolves along with the library, it is not possible to know everything upon graduating. Knowing where to access the resources to stay relevant to changing customer needs is key—even if it might move at a different pace than the library.

Regarding my co-worker Tara's comment, I think she was also questioning who and what defines that line. Is it always a smooth linear process ("in with the old, out with the new")? Or are there stops and starts along the way with tweaks and pivots happening before more than one person adopts a new thing? Is it always administration defining the line when requiring staff to complete a set of competencies based around databases or the catalog, for example? Throughout our experiences as staff, we are typically given a shared starting point of required knowledge according to the various software and hardware the library owns. It makes sense to be familiar with and able to navigate the systems the library has invested in to inform the customers better. Over time, new systems come on board, and we must update our knowledge once again.

Teen customers might push the envelope and ask the question, "What's in it for me?" regarding the library. They ask for the computers to access a popular online gaming platform, establish physical markers from the library to interface with the latest mobile augmented reality game, or even play the latest video game in pairs in the library. The librarians may decide to define the line ourselves. It is usually a combination. One thing for sure is that the line keeps changing. Do we chase after it, or do we watch it disappear until the next wave? What factors influence it? What are the repercussions of not doing anything? These are all great questions we will ponder throughout this chapter and this book. In the process, we will establish a foundation to embrace the line's impermanence and use it to help teens develop the skills they need to join the workforce or further a current interest.

DEFINING THE GENERATION

When I went to library school, one technology skill we learned was how to design a web page. It was not anything too attractive, using basic HTML coding. It did prove somewhat useful in various iterations of my career, but the library system I work for now has a web services department dedicated to this, so it is not something I do regularly. That is not uncommon for larger library systems. Even if designing a web page is part of your current job, the software you learned while in school has probably changed. The skills come in handy periodically when helping teens create their online portfolios. Still, nowadays, most editors are in a WYSIWYG format (What You See Is What You Get), which makes knowing the details of the HTML coding commands less necessary. The technology I am learning now focuses on graphic design using vector graphics and printing them on a T-shirt, which I never learned while in library school. The point is that technology is always evolving, and so we are continually learning how to do things differently.

1. What technology skills are essential to being a librarian and working with youth in your community today?
2. How can you use technology to reach new youth?
3. What kind of technology events can your organization support that might draw new youth to the library?

One way to better understand the landscape of youth and technology is through a generational lens. Sometimes, studying differing generations can make one generation feel justified in attributing problems to anyone but themselves. But each generation usually has a handful of overarching characteristics shaped by the cultural and political landscape in which they grew up. Technology invariably plays a starring role by intertwining itself or even driving these experiences to help further define a set of unique qualities. Who gets to define a generation based on what information is up for debate. In her recent book *iGen: Why Today's Super-Connected Kids Are Growing Up Less Rebellious, More Tolerant, Less Happy—and Completely Unprepared for Adulthood—and What That Means for the Rest of Us*,[2] psychologist Jean Twenge defines those born between 1995 and 2012 as the "iGens." This cohort is also known as "Gen Z" or the "Post-Millennials." These characteristics can be a starting place for understanding current teens and the role that technology plays in their lives.

Twenge states that they are named the "iGens" because "they grew up with cell phones, had an Instagram page before they started high school, and do not remember a time before the Internet." Much of her book becomes a slippery slope when she treats "correlation as causation." A review of Twenge's book in an article from NPR states that the book takes a negative view on the effects of technology and teen use.[3]

Twenge's data was gathered from national surveys conducted of more than 11 million teens since the 1960s. She found that due in part to the amount of time spent per day with media (approximately five to six hours), "new media is making teens more lonely, anxious, and depressed, and is undermining their social skills and even their sleep." She says that social media use equates with more screen time by nature and less time spent face-to-face with others. Girls are more vulnerable than boys because they report using social media more. These are mental health consequences that change the teen brain and make them "more emotional and more sensitive in the social world." On a less subtle note, she feels that teens are slower to grow up in the areas of postponing sex or hanging out with their parents.

Perhaps you have recognized these characteristics in some of the teens you interact with at the library. While many factors beyond technology can influence teens' emotional state from one day to the next or even one minute to the next, it raises a good question:

What is the library's role in interacting with teens and technology in this generation? More discussion and background need to take place to understand Twenge's explanations better. It is unlikely that everything undesirable in teens' lives can be reduced to one factor—technology (gaming, music, screen time). It is not necessarily the librarians' role to limit teen use of social media, but perhaps better understand the possibilities for positivity and balance through our interaction and use of it in the library.

LOCAL VIEW ON TEENS AND TECHNOLOGY

Now that we have a general understanding of teens and technology through a generational perspective, let us look at how local teens are powering up in and around the library. Teen access to and use of technology can be vastly different from one community or neighborhood to the next and one library to another.

A few years ago, my library system started putting more of its collection budget toward ebooks rather than print copies. I did not get a sense that very many teens at my branch owned ereaders or made a dramatic shift from print materials to online books. Many owned mobile devices, mostly phones, which, anecdotally, seemed primarily used for watching YouTube videos and interacting on social media (Facebook, Snapchat, Instagram) with their friends. Teens and preteens alike have their fair share of tablets, but they were used mostly to download the latest game (Pokémon Go, Walking Dead, Nintendo games). I did not have enough information to determine why ebooks' popularity with adults did not translate for teens at my branch. There were differences from one neighborhood to the next, where ebooks would prove to be a more popular format for teens. One size does not fit all. Your observations can be a great place to start to give you more information about teens and technology today. Even if it is a small sample, do not discount what you see. Do not make sweeping conclusions either. Observation is one more tool available to understand the library's role better.

Later in this chapter, we look at emerging technology trends organized into a few broad categories. These trends are based on several criteria. First is the persistence of the topic in the news and on social media. For example, in a Pew Internet Research Center survey in 2018, 95 percent of teens said they have or have access to a smartphone, representing a 22-percentage-point increase from the 73 percent of teens who said this in 2014 to 2015.[4] You may witness this in your library, which supports the data. It is a technology that is so common that it might feel odd to think about a phone as a tool to educate students on how to find information effectively. Another mark of a trend is that it has impacted the library field as a frequent topic on blogs, in journal articles, and frequently as a conference session. Lastly, the impact of a trend is far-reaching and goes well beyond the walls of the library.

EMERGING TECHNOLOGY TRENDS

In the summer of 2019, I attended an "Emerging Technology Trends in Libraries" workshop by David Lee King, the digital services director at Topeka and Shawnee County Public Library. He presented this workshop throughout the country through the Technology and Trends Roundtable with the North Carolina Library Association, which brought him to the Pack Memorial Library in Asheville, North Carolina, to speak. He addressed shaping an organization responsive to change through the lens of emerging trends around us and then in libraries themselves. The presentation organized technology into several categories and asked the question, "What does this mean for the library?" This perspective assumes that we cannot ignore the technology that is trending, and we should do something about it; as his opening slide read, "Technology is a given. Not a debate." I have replicated some of the categories of technology trends below. We will look at them through the use by young adults. It is an excellent opportunity for all readers to ask the question, "What does this mean for my library?"

TREND CATEGORIES

We will look at three public libraries—one rural, one urban, and one in between—to get a general snapshot of technology and spark some new ideas of serving teens at your library with technology. Just initiating conversations with library staff and teens can reenergize how we engage with youth in the community, and they, in turn, with the library. We will see how technology is used with teens, how it has changed over time, and how staff are responding to the changing landscape to keep the technology relevant for teens continually.

Belgrade Community Library, Montana

First, we will look at the Belgrade Community Library in Montana, named the 2015 Best Small Library in America by *Library Journal*.[5] Youth Services Librarian Benjamin Elliott projected the service area to be a bit over 13,000 people. Elliott said that the staff would expand to add a part-time circulation assistant in response to the growth of the population. There are nine staff, including the director, circulation specialists, and one library assistant, three more than just four years ago. Elliott has been the youth services librarian since the summer of 2019. As is with most positions, he inherited some projects already in place, whether through grants or customer interest. He started new programs himself based on current teen use of the library and what appeals to them. In 2017–2018, the Belgrade Community Library was one of the twenty-eight recipients of Google's Ready to Code grant through the American Library Association. Technology was purchased, including laptops, Raspberry Pis, and other peripherals for an after-school gaming group. In a partnership with students from nearby Montana State University in the engineering and computer science programs, the library hosted a series of programs with the teens. The current iteration of coding under Elliott's leadership is a combination STEAM program, including elementary school ages and families once a month.

The Montana State Library supports the circulation of technology kits to libraries throughout the state, such as LEGO Robotics, which can then be checked out via curriers to other libraries. There may be more technology available through this sharing model with the state library; Elliott is inventorying the resources as of this writing.

Elliott has his ear to the community and is aware of the teens' interests, either by observing program attendance or talking to them about their interests. He then adjusts the programs and experiences accordingly. He also uses the collection as a guide by noting which materials or topics get checked out the most often. Checking out materials on a particular topic does not necessarily correlate with program interest and attendance, as Elliott has found:

> The core group I have doesn't have coding and tech as one of their main interests right now. However, our books related to computer science and coding do get regular use. I've tried to gauge interest from some of the people who check these books out, and most of the teens interested in reading the books wanted to do their own thing and weren't interested in participating in special programs at the library.

Elliott adds that the teens who attend the most recent iteration of the coding club seem to do so because their parents strongly encourage them. While Elliott still wants to build up the number of teens that attend programs, he will have to continue to find new ways to do so, and so far he is doing all the right things. Preteens are currently the most attended age bracket that Elliott serves.

Spartanburg County Public Library, South Carolina

Next, we look at a middle-sized library and how technology is used with their teen population. We explore how staff are responding to the changing landscape to continually keep the technology relevant for teens.

Spartanburg County Public Library (SCPL), located in upstate South Carolina, is a nine-branch system plus a headquarters. The library plays a crucial role in strategically serving teens in the community. In a January 2020 email interview, Teen Services Librarian Travis Sanford shared that "teen services staff need to be responsive." One of the ways this is accomplished at Spartanburg County is by operating from a foundation where each branch employs a teen services assistant. Like most libraries with a teen department at each branch, the assistants are responsible for programming and maintaining the teen spaces. As part of the larger system, they contribute to initiatives such as the Teen Summer Reading program. A branch teen assistant differs in that they may have circulation duties and work more with the tween population. Lastly, there is a headquarters location where the director of teen services, assistant director of teen services, teen services librarian, and three teen services assistants work. Sanford explains that "at Headquarters, the staff is dedicated to serving teens, primarily planning programs and larger initiatives, acting in a support role to branch teen assistants, and staffing the Teen Hub, a recently remodeled space reserved just for teens." This model is worth considering if you are hoping to increase the support and workforce in the library to better serve teens in the community.

The Spartanburg County Public Library received a Library Services and Technology Act (LSTA) Summer Reading Grant from the South Carolina State Library in 2019. They used it to purchase a Cricut Maker[6] along with extra accessories. The Cricut is a portable device that can make vinyl projects, including stickers, signs, and designs on T-shirts. Each location was able to use the Cricut Maker in a program, and they have used it beyond summer reading as well, such as during winter break for teens to make stickers. Teens can use the Cricut Maker to create their brand or logo and decorate their laptops, skateboards, or coffee mugs.

About five years ago, SCPL was awarded an LSTA mini grant. Circulating kits were created that included devices such as Spheros, Ozobots, and littleBits. While many of these devices they purchased are still in use and relevant today, five years can be a long time regarding technology that gets old very quickly. Fortunately, SCPL contributed their programming monies to upgrade their STEAM offerings to include iPads, Oculus Go system for virtual reality, Sphero Mini Robots that are programmable via mobile devices, and Bloxels, which is a game design and interactive story builder program. Pooling resources into a kit that can circulate throughout a library system or consortium is a common model. If the resources are available to do so, it makes sense as a strategic way to reach a broader range of youth throughout the library's service area. It is an economical approach, not only by sharing the existing technologies but also sharing knowledge for programming—whether a lesson plan, group training, or best practices.

Charlotte Mecklenburg Library, North Carolina

Next, we take a snapshot of teens and technology within an extensive urban library system in Charlotte, North Carolina, which serves more than a million customers. The

Charlotte Mecklenburg Library (CML) has twenty branches and a digital branch; four have rooms that are dedicated makerspaces as of this writing. While chapter 9 goes more in depth on makerspaces, we mention briefly how that is defined particularly to this system. The working definition of a *makerspace* we are using in this book is that it is "any area where people gather to make and create."

ImaginOn, a branch in the system entirely dedicated to youth, also has Studio i, which focuses on filmmaking. It includes a blue screen, dress-up costumes, and a sound booth and keyboard for music recording.

Figure 1.1. Filming in front of the blue screen. *Photo by Kelly Czarnecki*

In 2016, an LSTA grant was awarded to the system to have mobile equipment called satellite studios that could live at three branches for some time. Resources such as a green screen, iMac computer, and keyboard with programming intended for all ages were included in the studios. Separate from the LSTA grant and the system through additional funding are kits used by staff that include Bloxels, a Sphero SPRK + Power Pack, ten iPads, ten Chromebooks, and an Ice Cream Ball, which teaches basic science principles while making ice cream.

Having a variety of ways that technology can be available, having the space for a room to be dedicated, or having something mobile and circulating are ways to work outside some of the limits we might have with funding or access. Many public libraries were designed or remodeled with a computer lab or at least space for computers somewhere. Making space for new technologies is something that libraries are frequently called to do to serve customers the best that we can.

At CML, all programs require an accompanying lesson plan and an educational component. A template of the lesson plan is included at the end of this chapter. This foundation ensures that the organization is providing quality services to the community. The lesson plans help streamline the process of presenting a program. If someone at a branch is unsure where to begin doing a particular program or might want to replicate one they heard was a great success, the lesson plan provides them with the information and links to do so. The lesson plans also help with the consistency of the delivery and performance of the program. While this might sound like a standardized approach, the information is delivered in a relaxed and informal manner.

CONCLUSION

As of this writing, every branch within the CML system has a dedicated teen services staff and a space dedicated to teens within the buildings. The young adult collection is in the teen space. Teen-friendly posters, displays, and signage showing that the area is intended for teens are on the walls or tables. Several branches are located close by or directly across from a school, which means an influx of youth after school. Computer labs fill up quickly with competing interests and rising noise levels from teens and adults. Some branches have computers in the teen space that can only be logged on with a library card within a specific age range, so teens are among their peers. Noise travels easily, so it is not always a perfect solution if the technology cannot be in a more enclosed space. As of this writing, video gaming is still a welcomed activity by teens at the library. Some branches offer the gaming as a scheduled program that is on the calendar and requires registration. In contrast, other branches have a dedicated space where some of the equipment, such as a TV screen, is on the wall, and hours for the youth to participate via signing up are posted.

Lesson Plan for: Click here to enter text.

Program Portal Catalog ID   Click here to enter text.
#:

Target Audience(s):	☐Older Adults Ages 65+	☐Adults Ages 19-64	☐Teens Ages 12-18
	☐Preteens Ages 10-11	☐School Age 5-11	☐Preschool Ages 3-5
	☐Toddlers Age 19-36 Months	☐Babies/Toddlers Ages 0-18 Months	☐Families

Focus Area: Choose an item.

Program Objective:

Click here to enter text.

Introduction:

Click here to enter text.

Closing:

Click here to enter text.

Program Time:

Preparation: Click here to enter text.   Remember that program planning includes tasks like developing/reviewing program curriculum, locating an outside presenter, shopping for program supplies, marketing the

Figure 1.2.   Lesson plan template.

program, printing out handouts for participants, and day-of tasks like the room set up and clean up for outreach programming, including travel time to and from the program.

Delivery: Click here to enter text.

Materials: Click here to enter text.

Procedure:

Click here to enter text.

Resources: (Pictures, links, etc.)

Click here to enter text.

Procedure formats.

Format A:

1:00-1:05 → Welcome program participants. Introduce the program with the objective(s).

1:05-1:15 → Talk about the first topic; include these relevant points:

1:15-1:30 → Lead a discussion with participants about the first topic; suggested questions include:

1:30-1:55 → Provide enough detail in each time block to guide the facilitator through the program if they are familiar with the topic's basic concepts.

Lesson plan template (continued).

1:55-2:00 → Wrap up the program by thanking participants for attending, recommending other library programs, services, or resources, and reminding them of the program's objective.

Format B:

A program that does not require the program facilitator to be actively engaged the entire time (i.e., an outside presenter is doing the bulk of the presentation) can be summarized with enough detail to provide the program facilitator enough information to facilitate the program easily. The program should begin with: Welcome program participants. Introduce the program with the objective(s). Wrap up the program by thanking participants for attending, recommending other library programs, services, or resources, and reminding them of the objective of the program.

Lesson plan template (continued).

NOTES

1. Kroski, Ellyssa. *The Makerspace Librarian's Sourcebook*. Chicago: American Library Association, 2017.
2. Twenge, Jean M. *iGen: Why Today's Super-Connected Kids Are Growing Up Less Rebellious, More Tolerant, Less Happy—and Completely Unprepared for Adulthood—and What That Means for the Rest of Us*. New York: Atria Books, 2018.
3. Quinn, Annalisa. "Move Over Millennials, Here Comes 'iGen' . . . Or Maybe Not." NPR. September 17, 2017. https://www.npr.org/2017/09/17/548664627/move-over-millennials-here-comes-igen-or-maybe-not.
4. Anderson, Monica, and Jingjing Jiang. "Teens, Social Media & Technology 2018." Pew Research Center: Internet & Technology. May 31, 2018. https://www.pewresearch.org/internet/2018/05/31/teens-social-media-technology-2018/.
5. "Belgrade Community Library Named the 2015 Best Small Library in America by the Library Journal." Belgrade Community Library. January 28, 2015. https://www.belgradelibrary.org/library-journal-names-belgrade-community-library-the-2015-best-small-library-in-america/.
6. Cricut Home. Accessed September 30, 2020. http://www.cricut.com/.

TWO
Technology Setup

The physical space of the library—school or public—plays a role in how teens interact with technology, as does the setup for virtual programming when connecting with teens outside of the library. We explore the broader questions about access to technology and how libraries can play a role through partnerships in furthering those connections. An IT representative or a local organization can help secure your network when setting up a bank of wired computers.

This chapter offers tips to freshen up already existing library spaces and how to start from scratch. We look at technology from the viewpoints of being in a teens-only space at the library and shared spaces, such as a computer lab. There may be opportunities to provide an environment that meets teens' needs in shared spaces through suggested structures or policies. We draw on several resources, including our own experiences. YALSA's *Teen Space Guidelines* is a free "tool for evaluating a public library's overall level of success in providing physical and virtual space dedicated to teens, aged 12–18."[1] The space for teens may be in a public or school library or a designated remote learning center, which we have seen more of during the pandemic, offering youth Wi-Fi, staffing, or volunteers and supplies to learn. It is important and helpful to understand that the library's environment can foster the positive development of customers' social and emotional needs. It is not unusual to see shelving in the children's section that is an accessible height to select their materials. Seating by wide-open windows is optimal for any age to find inspiration and quiet to study. Teens are no different from any other customer when needing a space that reflects their needs. If constructing from the ground up, remodeling an existing space, or addressing some challenges within the space due to unanticipated use, such as the need for a noise barrier or more comfortable seating, it is common to visit other libraries. If you are unable to visit other spaces physically, then request a virtual visit appointment. You can ask more probing questions beyond what you might have viewed in an article and can also see a space in more detail. Concerning technology as part of the space, ask about the resources you might not readily see. For example, technology usually goes beyond the bank of networked computers or laptops for checkout.

1. Are there items such as robots, circuitry kits, or other tools that you might consider purchasing for checkout and use in the library?
2. How does the library build for change and innovation?

Figure 2.1. Sphero robotics maze. *Photo by Kelly Czarnecki*

BUILDING FOR CHANGE

Because technology changes so rapidly, even without a pandemic, it is vital to build for change. Even though the shift to virtual programming and instruction for many libraries was an abrupt change in 2020, it may have forced movement in ways we already desired to interact. For example, while using IG Live or Instagram Live—which is streaming a real-time video with or without multiple people—it is not uncommon to interact with followers. Previously, it was not the primary way most libraries interacted with customers. Now that there are fewer options available to connect in person, it became a more popular means. After the pandemic, it is an opportunity to reach out on our social media accounts as a program or promotion. It is great to reframe our mindset and realize that these new ways we may have been forced to use technology may have utility beyond the pandemic. Being able to pivot no matter what our job or circumstances is also a useful skill to have. Job descriptions need to include familiarity with new technologies the library offers for customers and time to support employees' knowledge and exploration.

Another way to accommodate change with setting up the technology is to make everything as mobile as possible, from the tables that the computers rest on to a makerspace on a cart with wheels. Ask the organizations you reach out to what they wish they would have done differently. It may have a simple solution, such as moving a 3D printer to a different location to gain more interest, or it may be something more complicated that doesn't have a quick fix.

If possible, encourage teens to participate in a virtual meeting to give their input on what they like about the space or what they would change, and invite them to share some stories about what they do when they come to the library. Are there youth who have been a part of the library who can speak about changes or adaptations made, such as additional funding, partnerships, or technology due to their use?

BEYOND THE LIBRARY

Take into consideration various teen spaces in the community, especially those focused on technology, which is what we want to integrate. Consider virtual visits to gather ideas if it is not practical to visit. Here are some suggestions to get you started:

Museums

Some museums have a robust technology component and are not necessarily limited to those focusing on STEM. Engaging youth in understanding more about the museum through gameplay or after-school workshops can give insight into how exhibits are set up to encourage interaction (or not), discovery, and curiosity.

Retail

While the mall's popularity may be a thing of the past, stores specializing in technology still depend on teens and other consumers to purchase their products. The music these stores play, the lighting, how gadgets are secured yet allow for touch and play—all of this is valuable information. Larger screens for viewing presentations and mobile and functional seating can attract audience members that want to drop in. What aspects, if any, of the setup of a retail store might you want to replicate at your library?

Online Platforms

See where teens are online and what they do there by asking them. You do not need to set up an account to be online with them, but you may need to seek out organizations that will let you come and ask the teens questions and observe. Are they talking animatedly to one another while they are online? This indicates the need for comfortable seating and a place where they can be talkative and not interrupt others. Is being a spectator part of the whole experience? Having a large screen and extra seating might be something to accommodate this in the library space.

Community Centers

Neighborhood hangouts that attract youth after school or on weekends, such as the local YMCA, Boys and Girls Club, or other space, can all be locations to scope out ideas. Seeing what teens gravitate toward and learning what policies govern the space and what has changed over time can give insight into how you may want to design your area. Do not discount visiting places either virtually or in person that are farther away from your library and attract a different demographic. Exposure may help you identify how to be more inclusive in your own space and draw in the youth you do not often see.

Makerspaces fall into this category as well, which we talk more about in chapter 9. The technology itself does not define a makerspace, yet the setup is critical. How the space is laid out to encourage (or discourage) use can determine if people will feel moved to create. Safety balanced with creativity and order can make or break a space. Policies can drive these fundamentals, as can the physical layout.

Other Types of Libraries

Look at other types of libraries in your community that have a youth space or offer youth services different from your library. You may even have a nearby college or university with robust technology resources as part of their library or makerspace. Policies and practice around checking out items and balancing security with experimentation can be useful information on how you might want to implement this in your location.

Technology plays an important role in teens' social and emotional needs. We are going to examine physical and virtual space to integrate technology for teens and libraries. If you start with the idea that the technology can be moveable and not anchored to the floor, you will have a much better time supporting its adjustment when changing things around. One of the main factors that can influence the need to shift things is customers. Dr. Anthony Bernier, author and professor, notes a phenomenon called "The Geography of No!" where libraries create spaces and force teens into behaviors that contradict how they actually work.[2] If the gaming area is not utilized because teens are in uncomfortable chairs or are always told to be quiet from customers in an adjacent department, you probably want to reconfigure some furniture or add sound buffers, such as moveable whiteboard walls that double as graffiti boards.

If you are fortunate enough to be involved in starting a teen space from scratch, do your research. You may not feel completely comfortable in knowing how the latest social networking site is utilized by teens, but do not feel so paralyzed that you are not letting your voice be heard at the table. Leverage your ability as a community connector, a teen advocate, and a researcher to help build the space for the present and the capacity for the future.

VIRTUAL PROGRAMMING

How libraries look will continue to develop in response to the changing landscape. At the time of this writing, library services look different in the reopening phases of the pandemic than they did in early 2020. Library outreach has been a service delivery model in my system and many others across the country for years. A bookmobile or staff go to a location because that may be the only way to connect to customers who might not have transportation, are incarcerated, or are even physically unable to come to the brick-and-mortar locations. Virtual outreach is not unheard of in my system, as well as many others. The degree that it has been used to provide programming during the pandemic has shifted to almost 100 percent. Inequities are experienced by those who cannot have reliable internet access or a device that allows them to connect, which needs to be addressed. Recording a session can open opportunities for convenience to participate in a virtual program or even attend later. Even though it is not a replacement for human contact, virtual programming may continue to have a more significant role even after the pandemic in engaging customers alongside more traditional ways. We have developed and perfected how to do so and are reaching a customer base that we might not otherwise be able to.

Delivering virtual programming was not a simple switch to move the same services to the popular Zoom platform or other sites such as Facebook or Instagram Live. A patchwork of closures, lockdowns, and phased-in services in 2020 due to the pandemic thrust most libraries into rethinking many traditional services during a crisis. Teen programming was no different. We needed to respond to the cracks revealed in the social infrastructure that validated the history of how libraries in the United States came to be and were not always welcoming spaces for all. One such undertaking in serving teens during the pandemic has been through a series of posts with *School Library Journal* and virtual sessions through a program titled *Rethinking Youth Librarianship* with Mega M. Subramaniam and Linda W. Braun. The direction of the dialogue within the program stated, "Rather than simply shifting existing programs to an online format" our goal needs to be "how to connect with the community to determine critical services."[3] The topics shed light on structures that may not have included the full depth of what the community needed at first, the disparities of which the pandemic exposed. For example, the social justice issues that rose to the surface during the pandemic when schools were nearing the end of the 2020 school year, which was operating remotely, left many students offline—we may not know the real effect for a while.

The amount of time to prepare for the shift was minimal, not allowing for a medium not previously used or supported widely by the staff or library. For many libraries, focusing on access to "stuff" such as handling and sanitizing materials or social distancing signage came at the expense of focusing on whom the library serves. "Yes, our fellow citizens need ebooks, but they need compassion, connection, and community dedicated to their full well-being,"[4] as Subramaniam and Braun say. Many of us provided what we could, given the situation, but at the same time, such a reactionary response also closed off some possibilities for connection with youth.

Before COVID closures, it was not unusual for libraries to make available mobile technology to check out. School, academic, and public libraries saw a need and provided a way to get technology in the hands of those who wanted to use it. For example, hot spots, video cameras, chargers, or laptops have long been part of the array of materials that can be accessed with a library card and checked out by customers at some libraries. Internal staff use of the equipment, whether for programming, promoting a program or service, or creating content for a digital branch, is also an option at some libraries. During COVID closures in the United States starting in the early spring of 2020, public libraries could continue programming virtually. Using various social media platforms such as Zoom, Instagram, and Facebook, book discussions and presentations transitioned online more naturally than other programs. Gaming may have taken a different skill set or networking with those already familiar with a particular game such as Dungeons & Dragons or Animal Crossing.

As a result of the programming shift, more equipment may have been needed and purchased for internal use if funds were available, mainly because more staff were using it at once. For example, the following is an example of what was purchased for a single branch to share and facilitate programming for adults, teens, and children's divisions. You may want to consider some of the purchases even if we are no longer in a "phased reopening" during COVID. While virtual learning should not be a complete replacement for in-person interaction, some benefits may warrant continuing the service, such as reaching those who are unable to come to the library. It may be easier scheduling-wise as a type of outreach event (for you and attendees). It can be easier on the environment if you do not have to drive everywhere. It can also be a way to bring people together who might not otherwise easily come in contact with one another and a way to connect customers with the library, ideas, and other people.

An example of a systemwide equipment purchase to support online programming at a public library includes the following from the Charlotte Mecklenburg Library system. It was purchased in the middle of the summer of 2020, several months after the library was closed due to COVID. The list is rather general and reflects the availability of products when virtual learning and meeting, when it went widespread in a short amount of time, was starting. Since then, new practices and equipment have likely been made more available as the needs of the community change. Nevertheless, the list below can give you helpful information on what to consider when doing programming setup intended as a virtual stage for customers to participate with you. Depending on the size of the branch, there may have been multiple kits included. The intent was that the equipment was shared within a branch for adult, teen, and children's services programming. The prices shown reflect what was purchased at the time through Best Buy or Amazon and totaled around $200. Whether a phone or tablet, the main projecting devices were already assumed to be owned, having been purchased previously for the library system, but will be the most expensive items to purchase if needed.

- Tripod to hold the recording device, such as a smartphone. An adapter to hold a tablet such as an iPad was also included. Cost: $75
- Tablet mount that works with the tripod and tablet. Cost: $40
- Clip-on microphone that plugs into a smartphone or tablet (via the headphone jack) for better audio quality. If using an iPhone or iPad, a headphone/lightning adapter is included in this kit. Cost: $40
- iPhone/lightning converter that will allow the clip-on mic to plug into an Apple device that does not have a headphone jack. Cost: $8
- Lighting kit that includes light stands, bulbs, a carrying bag, an umbrella reflector, and a manual. Everything needed to light the filming of the program. Cost: $55

These are just some general ideas to get started with technology setup for virtual programming. Tech setup does not have to be daunting or overbearing. If it is approached with the attitude and capacity to allow for change based on customer usage and ever-growing technology, you will be that much more poised to ride the waves as they come.

NOTES

1. *Teen Space Guidelines*. Young Adult Library Services Association (YALSA). November 10, 2017. http://www.ala.org/yalsa/guidelines/teenspaces.

2. Bernier, Anthony. "The Case against Libraries as 'Safe Places.'" 2003. *Voice of Youth Advocates (VOYA)*, 26: 198–99.

3. Braun, Linda W., and Mega M. Subramaniam. "Retire Those Legacy Approaches. It's Time to Be Bold and Innovative: Reimagining Libraries." *School Library Journal*. July 7, 2020. Accessed September 30, 2020. https://bit.ly/2CqYLXw.

4. Subramaniam, Mega M., and Linda W. Braun. "COVID-19 Is an Opportunity to Rethink Youth Librarianship: Reimagining Libraries." *School Library Journal*. May 31, 2020. Accessed September 30, 2020. https://www.slj.com/?detailStory=covid-19-is-an-opportunity-to-rethink-youth-librarianship-reimagining-libraries.

THREE
Funding Technology

Before going into more detail concerning different technologies that you might consider for your library, let us pause to consider how to fund these purchases. Like many library professionals across the nation, you recognize that your patrons' needs are continually evolving and changing. You must adapt your budget to make appropriate technology purchases. You may have found yourself daydreaming of products you could purchase or programs you could plan if only you had more funding. Or maybe you know that there are more funds available if you can make a clear argument to your supervisor or director.

Many libraries receive funding from a variety of sources. For example, your library might receive a large portion of funding from a tax levy, supplemented with funds from a Friends of the Library group. Your library may be funded mostly by the city with supplemental funds from grants and fundraising. American libraries have been steadily losing funding due to budget decreases coupled with inflation and aggravated by an "information explosion" that asks libraries to purchase more and more materials with decreasing budgets.[1] With an ever-increasing number of articles and books published both traditionally and via independent sources each year, libraries feel pressure to purchase a larger volume of materials. On top of the expected purchases, libraries also fund technology purchases that help prepare teens for further education and employment and bridge the digital divide.

This chapter explores the different ways in which library funds are sourced: namely, funding from city, county, or state government; Friends of the Library groups; fundraisers; and grants. Each section will also include advice on approaching these sources for additional funds as needed.

CITY, COUNTY, OR STATE GOVERNMENT FUNDS

Many public libraries and public school libraries receive a portion of their budget from various government levels. For example, a public library in Small Town, Oklahoma, may receive funds from Small Town, Small Town County, Oklahoma, and the United States. The chart that follows shows the origin of funding, per capita, for the average public library. In most cases, a majority of funding (approximately 88 percent) comes from the local government, which includes the town or city and the county in which the library is situated. States and the federal government contribute the remaining needed funds, often in the form of grants.

While it is wonderful that public libraries can receive so much funding from government sources, it leaves libraries vulnerable to economic recessions. In the same report from the IMLS (Institute of Museum and Library Services), funding had continued to be lower than expected following the Great Recession of 2008–2009. The report says that funding is moving back toward pre-recession levels, but at a more sluggish rate than before.

It is up to each county or city to determine how to establish and fund public libraries. In some locations, a major city might partner with the county in which it resides to support a system of public libraries throughout the county. In other instances, a major city may form a separate library or library system without the county. For example, the Multnomah Public Library system serves the large city of Portland, Oregon, with branch locations throughout the county. In contrast, Los Angeles, California, has separate library systems for Los Angeles and the rest of the county. In areas with less dense populations, there may be even a third system called a conglomerate. In this scenario, multiple smaller counties may join together to best finance a public library system with branches throughout the region. A benefit to this option is that all libraries in the region may share a collection, making a larger selection of materials available to cardholders. In all cases, local governing bodies create and approve budgets and then share them with the library. These budgets often define the allowed uses of the funds; in other words, a certain amount is to be used to purchase materials only, another amount is to be spent on programs for the public, and so on. The amount of the budget dedicated to technology or youth services would be available for technology purchases. These budgets tend to expire at the end of the fiscal year, meaning that they must be spent in full or else the library loses the excess. The next section will cover Friends of the Library and other nonprofit library support groups, where libraries can pull funds that may be more discretionary to spend.

Public libraries are supported only in small part by the federal government. The Institute of Museum and Library Services is the department that administers the distribution of federal funds to public libraries, and they do so through the Library Services and Technology Act (LSTA). Last updated in 2018, the IMLS and LSTA continue to work together to promote public libraries' growth in America with a distribution of $6.2 million in 2020.[2] The federal funds operate in much the same way any other grants function in that a library must apply for the funds and then manage the grant and track any results

Indicator	FY 2015	FY 2014[i]
Indicator 1. Total Operating Revenue per Capita	$39.94	$39.77
Indicator 1.1 Operating Revenue per Capita from Local Government	$34.16	$33.87
Indicator 1.2 Operating Revenue per Capita from State Government	$2.83	$2.80
Indicator 1.3 Operating Revenue per Capita from Federal Government	$0.14	$0.15
Indicator 1.4 Operating Revenue per Capita from Other Sources	$2.80	$2.94
Indicator 2. Total Operating Expenditures per Capita	$37.38	$37.36
Indicator 2.1 Operating Expenditures per Capita on Staffing	$24.98	$25.03
Indicator 2.2 Operating Expenditures per Capita on Collections	$4.21	$4.20
Indicator 2.3 Operating Expenditures per Capita on Other Costs	$8.18	$8.13

[i] In constant 2015 dollars.

NOTE: Per capita estimates in the table use the unduplicated population. Calculations are based on unrounded estimates; therefore, reported totals may differ due to rounding.

SOURCE: IMLS, Public Libraries Survey, FY 2014–2015.

Figure 3.1. Funding for public libraries. *Institute of Museum and Library Services. "Public Libraries in the United States Fiscal Year 2015." 2018. Accessed June 19, 2020. https://www.imls.gov/sites/default/files/publications/documents/plsfy2015.pdf*

from it. Funds are granted to state libraries from the federal government, and then local libraries can apply to their state library for grants for specific projects. Each state library website contains the necessary information for an application, including the types of eligible programs, total maximum amounts awarded, page limits, any required matching funds, and examples of previous winning projects. If not required, many states encourage that projects benefit the library as a whole rather than benefiting one individual branch of a library. Because a library system is less likely to win more than one grant and because of the preference for projects with large impacts, a library system should work together to apply. If your library is fortunate to have a dedicated grant writer, this staff member would be a valuable resource for research and wording.

Librarians work with their supervisor, director, and financial leader to request extra funds from local or state sources, annually and through a formal budget creation process. Your supervisor, director, or financial leader would be able to share details of this process and the parameters within which they can make a request.

FRIENDS OF THE LIBRARY AND OTHER FUNDRAISING GROUPS

Friends of the Library groups help provide funds to many libraries across the nation. In fact, in 1979, a Friends of the Libraries USA national organization was founded and is still housed in the American Library Association headquarters in Chicago, Illinois. This national organization provides guidance and support to the thousands of individual Friends of the Library groups.[3] These volunteer groups range in size, organization, and the amount of money that they can contribute, but they all produce a fair amount of energy and advocacy for their libraries. One library in Swissvale, Pennsylvania, credits their Friends group with making the public library as much a community center as a place to borrow books. The library director said, in 2014,

> Their events are a lot of fun. Everyone loves to come. And if it weren't for the money they raise, we'd have just a bare-bones budget for children's programs. The Friends also buy larger items as needed, like bookcases and carpeting. They contribute energy and ideas. They're a strong volunteer group, and we're very thankful for them.[4]

Friends groups everywhere provide community engagement and fundraiser opportunities through such events as bake sales or book sales, sometimes raising as much as tens of thousands of dollars annually. Many Friends groups are well organized enough to have successfully applied for and maintain a 501(c)(3) status with the IRS.

Friends of the Library groups are organized by charter and governed by bylaws. They will have a head or president of the group and governing board members. Nearly any community member can become a Friends of the Library member by indicating their support and paying membership dues. (Some Friends groups allow adults only to join and some Friends groups allow junior, or youth, members.) Each Friends group may decide upon their operating procedures as far as how often they convene, how to take votes, how to receive funding requests, and how often to give funds to the library they support. Because they are a separate entity from the library, often with their own 501(c)(3) status, they collect funds throughout the year via donations, memberships, and fundraisers in their own bank account and transfer money periodically to the library.

A second type of fundraising group established to support libraries is the endowment. Like Friends of the Library groups, endowment committees are formed as separate entities from the library they support. However, they are formed for the express purpose of raising funds and overseeing the pursuant bank account. Think of an endowment committee as you would a group in charge of a trust. These groups always have a 501(c)(3) status either independently or through an umbrella foundation organization. Further, they do not always have the same impetus to advocate or volunteer at the library they support. Their support can be provided solely through the funds they provide to the library. Endowment committees are governed by bylaws and may have limits on membership and roles.

Endowments begin with a robust fundraising campaign. This campaign establishes the principal corpus, or the amount that your endowment will grow off. The principal corpus is then invested in an account that will allow for moderate growth year after year in interest. Many endowments have bylaws that restrict the use of the principal corpus. For example, an endowment may begin with a campaign to raise $200,000. Once that goal is met, any additional funds raised and any interest earned on the initial $200,000 are available funds for access. There must always be at least $200,000 in the account.

Requesting funds from a Friends of the Library group or an endowment will work slightly differently in every library or library system. Your supervisor, director, or financial leader will be able to guide the way to request funds from your endowment. Unlike a request to your local or state government, requests to Friends or endowments can usually be made throughout a fiscal year without needing to wait for a single point in the budget cycle. Also, these funds are not always earmarked for specific uses. While some endowments may be set aside for the sole purpose of renovations or construction, for the most part, endowments and Friends funds are unrestricted.

FUNDRAISING

Fundraising is a short-term method for getting the necessary funds for technology purchases. Fundraising events are in addition to already having an existing Friends of the Library or endowment group. You would need an account to handle the influx of donations or purchases. Because most libraries are considered public entities connected strongly to local government, if not officially an entity under local government control, they cannot fundraise directly. However, your Friends group or endowment group can host a fundraising project or event for you, receive the funds, and then transfer the funds directly into the library's account for use. Fundraisers can take on many different sizes and shapes and be undertaken by libraries and library support groups of all sizes and locales. Some popular and common ideas include donation drives, special events, book sales, and naming of buildings, spaces, or collections.

Donation drives can range from simple (placing marked containers on countertops in library branches) to more coordinated (online campaigns for donations and targeted requests to specific entities). It costs a library very little to place lockable plexiglass donation collection boxes in library branches; it costs nothing to place repurposed containers for donations. There are no major talking points for library frontline staff to deliver, and donations can be collected and tallied at the end of each day along with all other cash from the branch. Donation drives can be extended for any period of time: they can run until a predetermined amount is collected or can be a perennial source of extra income. If a library has the means to expand the donation drive slightly, they could include the ability for patrons to give online. Many fundraising websites can host a fundraiser for any person or organization. If your library is already set up to take online payments for fines and fees, they may add on the ability to take donation payments as well. To truly get the maximum impact from your drive, your library may also make targeted individual asks for donations of local businesses or corporations. This type of fundraising is simple and easily expandable to meet your library's needs.

Special events, single or recurring, are another popular fundraiser for libraries. A successful special fundraising event creates an air of exclusivity and promises entertainment. Examples of special fundraiser events include dinners, author appearances, silent auctions, or early access. For any of these events, the library would limit attendance by selling tickets. The attendees then know that their ticket grants them exclusive access, and the library knows that they will not run out of space. When people have to purchase entrance to an event, they are less likely to cancel at the last minute. Ticket sales are only the first part of these fundraisers. Once at the event, there are additional opportunities for patrons to give to the library. At a dinner, there will be a request and envelopes on the tables; at author appearances, there may be a request, or there may be book sales with profits returning to the library; at silent auctions, the items are donated, and all bids go to the library; and at early-access events, the participants purchase items during that time. Special events require more work from library staff to complete, but they also net more in return than donation drives.

Book sales are almost synonymous with library fundraising, as many libraries nationwide host annual, biannual, or continual book sales of donated or weeded materials. This fundraiser idea is scalable to the size of your library and its resources. Larger libraries or library systems may have the means to store six months' or one year's worth of donations and weeded materials and the space in which to host a large book sale over a weekend. Large sales require having storage space, hosting space, and a cadre of volunteers to set up and manage the sale. Libraries lacking in external storage could host book sales more frequently and store materials within library branches, or set up a continual book sale corner within each library branch. There are advantages to either book sale style; the large events garner attention and marketing and do not require much staff or volunteer attention outside of the event's weekend. The smaller continual book sale area within library branches does need staff or volunteers to restock and rotate material but is accessible for purchases year-round. Often Friends of the Library groups are in charge of book sales of any size or shape.

Naming is a fundraising type that is limited in scope and best handled by a library financial leader. Many libraries have plaques that indicate to patrons that the building as a whole, a particular space within the building, or a specific portion of the collection is in honor of a person's memory. Think of every library named [Last Name] Memorial Library or every plaque reading "Children's Picture Book Collection Given in Honor of [Beloved Children's Librarian]." Naming is not a fundraiser that is often advertised with open solicitation. It may be tied to the library's estate planning or arranged individually with the person or persons in charge of charitable giving at your library. It may also be part of the request to a person or corporation when approached for large gifts for specific purposes. For these reasons, it is best to work directly with your library's finance office if you are thinking of utilizing this form of fundraising for your technology purchase.

Working with your financial leader and your Friends of the Library group, fundraisers such as donation drives, special events, book sales, and naming rights are good ways to procure library funding for technology or technology programming.

GRANTS

Grants are a source of funding for libraries that supplement what is regularly promised in annual budgets from counties, states, or institutions. These infusions of funds most typically require an application to qualify, are finite, and require reporting on use. Grants are probably one of the most sought-after sources of funding, and competition can be fierce. For this reason, many library systems employ a professional grant writer whose full-time job is to research, write, and track grants for their library. This person works closely with frontline staff members to determine needs and then seek grants to meet those needs. Once a grant is secured, they continue to work closely with the staff in utilizing the funds and tracking their use and outcome. It is not always widely known that many grants require reporting. Sometimes it is assumed that a grant is "free money." However, most grant sources require library staff to report on the funds' use and outcomes. Honest reporting, even if the outcomes are not entirely as expected, can create credibility with the grant source and lead to future grant approvals.

In research for this book, an optional survey was distributed to many teen-serving library professionals. Nearly half of the respondents, 41 out of 96, said they rely on grants for at least a portion of their library technology purchases. It may be daunting to hear that so many of your library colleagues need to rely on grants above and beyond standard budgets for technology projects. Still, you can also take heart in knowing that they are successful in their applications and can use grants to fund technology.

One respondent, Sonya Moon, replied with excitement that she had just secured a $105,000 grant; $77,000 had been earmarked for a part-time staff member, and another $30,000 was for the creation of a robotics lab within her library. In a follow-up, Sonya shared further details of the process for the readers of this book. The following conversation will give a clear idea of what to expect when applying for and then receiving a grant.

Congratulations on your grant award! Did you write the application, or does your library system employ a grant writer? Either way, what types of sources did you consult in preparation for the writing? "No, I do all my own grants and have done many over the years. I think a grant writer would be a great idea, but it is not something we do. The grant we went for was a local Tasmanian one, so the people making the decisions already knew my community pretty well. That does help. My sources were mainly through partnerships, discussions we were already having about the demand for these types of programs, discussions with teachers who now have the digital curriculum included at schools, discussions with our local university and primary and high schools who deliver in this area about outside school provision. It was also parent/grandparent driven, as parents wanted to learn about the equipment and have opportunities for shared experiences with their child."

Can you share a little about the timeline? I want to set our readers up for reasonable expectations. How much time did you spend in research, how much in writing, how long before funds were released, and how long did you spend planning the project? "We had been offering programs for a good couple of years, and the demand was growing. The grant wasn't overly onerous, but we are fortunate that the funding body actually allows and gives you feedback on your draft. I had to be more specific with outcomes and really show exactly what I was going to deliver for the money. Vague did not cut it. I think I really underestimated the planning part of the project. The grant application was fairly straightforward, about ten hours of work, and then I set up a small advisory group of experts who supported me with what sort of equipment we would put in the application to purchase, etc. They work in various areas, including private enterprise, university level, community robotics programs, a teacher in primary and a teacher in high school digital skills, youth work at the local council, and ex Code Club Manager. Once successful, the funding body advised not to progress anything until we received funds, so this was a bit of a holding pattern. I did some background work and ordered some supplies but not too much planning."

What metrics do you expect to track and report back to the grant funder? "I presume you mean stats here. We will report on the number of participants, children, and adults, and they are in age groups from 3 through to 15. We shall report on geographical location (in a small municipality). I had to set targets in my funding application on how many would directly benefit from the project. Part of the project is a robotics library, so I will also report on loans once this gets up and running. (We are completely shut down at the moment due to COVID-19.) Very unfortunate as the project was going gangbusters, and we were offering a lot of programs. I had to cancel 40 when we closed: it was heartbreaking. So much work!"

Is there anything else I have failed to ask that you'd like to share with our future readers and me? "My big takeaway would be to try and cost in staffing. We costed in a project officer for 12 months at half time, 18 hours per week approximately at a Band 3 Customer Service Officer level, about $40AU per hour. The staffing has been a challenge to attract someone half time, who can do delivery to out of hours groups, in hours to parent groups, child care centers, homeschoolers, and admin. We haven't managed to get the balance just right as yet, and before closing, I had five people working in the project in part-time capacities. I do a lot more admin and planning of classes than I would like and can't really see this improving. As part of the funding, we were required to provide in-kind project management, which I do for an estimated 10 hours per month. It has realistically with programming been more like 10 hours per week. If I had my time again, I would have costed in a full-time project officer."[5]

Applying for and then managing grants is a large task. As seen in the preceding interview, library staff need to have a plan before applying for a grant and consider the cost of the materials and space and the cost of managing the project or space. Grants can be an excellent supplement to your budget. As you consider grants to apply for, weigh the possible additional money against the cost of time to apply and manage. Your library supervisor, director, or financial leader can help advise.

CONCLUSION

Funding for your technology purchases is going to come from your local, state, or federal government; Friends of the Library or other fundraising groups; your fundraising efforts; and grants. It is recommended that you work under your library director or financial leader's advice when seeking access to these funds. The portion of your budget from local, state, or federal government will likely be set entirely at the beginning of your fiscal year. Still, the end of the fiscal year brings an opportunity to make special or additional requests. Funds can be requested from Friends or other fundraising groups throughout the year via your library's process for doing so. With approval, you can put on a fundraiser of your own or apply for a grant throughout the fiscal year. These options will provide the means necessary to find the money for technology purchases for your library.

NOTES

1. Potts, Janet Christine, and Vincent Roper. (1995). "Sponsorship and Fund Raising in Public Libraries: American and British Perceptions." *New Library World*, 96(1): 13–22. https://doi.org/10.1108/03074809510075470.
2. Hines, Shawnda. "FY 2020 Library Budget Signed: Final Bill Includes Increases for LSTA and Other Programs." ALA American Library Association. December 20, 2019. Accessed June 20, 2020. http://www.ala.org/news/press-releases/2019/12/fy-2020-library-budget-signed-final-bill-includes-increases-lsta-and-other.
3. Potts and Roper. "Sponsorship and Fund-Raising in Public Libraries," 13.
4. Weisberg, Deborah. "'Friends' Are Hidden Backbone of Many Libraries in Pittsburgh, Elsewhere." *Pittsburgh Tribune-Review*. December 19, 2014. http://nclive.org/cgi-bin/nclsm?url=http://search.proquest.com/docview/1638455554?accountid=13217.
5. Moon, Sonya. Interview by Kelly Czarnecki. Email. May 3, 2020.

FOUR
Aligning Technology Programs with Your Library's Mission

Improve lives and build a stronger community.
—Charlotte Mecklenburg Library [1]

The mission of the library is to foster community and enrich the lives of individuals through learning, engagement, and connection.
—Beaverton City Library [2]

Charleston County Public Library connects our diverse community to information, fosters lifelong learning, and enriches lives.
—Charleston County Public Library [3]

We are the "People's University," the center of learning for a diverse and inclusive community.
—Cleveland Public Library [4]

To champion literacy, inspire learning, and foster community connection.
—Greenville County Library [5]

MISSION STATEMENTS

Everything done in your library aligns with a mission statement, and these mission statements exist to help guide what programs and services the library offers. Rebecca Nous excellently illustrated the purpose of a mission statement in a short allegory:

> Three people were at work on a construction site. All were doing the same job, but when each was asked what his job was, the answers varied. "Breaking rocks," replied the first. "Earning a living," answered the second. "Helping to build a cathedral," said the third.[6]

The third construction worker is the unknowing author of the group's mission statement. Whether they are breaking up rocks, showing up to collect a paycheck, or moving the broken rocks into place, they are all working toward the goal of creating a cathedral.

Mission statements are critically important to keeping business, organizations, and schools focused. They help to define your library's purpose and inspire both staff and customers. Passionate people can have many ideas as to the best programs or services to offer to their customers. It can be easy to become focused only on the customers nearest you and provide the services they request. For example, a teen-serving library staff member at a rural library branch may repeatedly hear from their customers that they desire meeting room space for 4-H meetings and programs that support vocational skills acquisition. That rural library branch may be part of a library system that serves the entire county, including many urban and suburban locations. Those locations may have customers who are clamoring for different programs. A mission statement can tie together the various activities, eliminate programs that are not serving the vision, and ensure that they are all working together toward a common goal, all of which strengthens the efficacy of the library. Being overly diverse in your programs can be a poor use of funds instead of focusing on those programs that the library already does well and that benefit the community.

Typically, the library's governing board, sometimes with input from library leadership, develops mission statements. Mission statements guide, define, and inspire a library for its duration. They can be revisited to update language, but should only be rewritten completely if the organization changes its focus entirely. Organizational goals and community needs are considered when writing the mission statement.

Organizational goals play a large part in the foundation of the mission statement. For public libraries, these goals may be set with the input of city or county council members; school libraries may have goals that correlate to the school's goals, and academic libraries will have goals that align with the overall institution's goals. The writers of the mission statement look at what the library hopes to accomplish or provide during a given period, and those goals become the foundation of the statement. As you plan programs and services and make purchases for your department, consider organizational goals. Organizational goals are the base for writing mission statements as well as informing programming and purchasing decisions.

Along with organizational goals, the community's needs should also be considered when writing a mission statement. Ask yourself what your library can and should provide for the community it serves. While the details of this answer may change over time, broader goals will not. For example, a mission of teaching JavaScript at all libraries may have been a great goal at the turn of the century. Now, however, teaching C++ or Python would be a better goal. This mission also fails to consider all of the customers who would prefer to enter a nontechnical vocation. Instead, you will want to write a broader mission statement: make it your library's goal to provide educational resources for all customers' passions. That statement will not age and covers all interests of your community. A library may also look at community needs to determine what programs or services should be provided and include those in their mission or vision statement.

PROGRAMMING GUIDELINES

Many libraries establish programming guidelines in addition to their mission statement. These guidelines further define parameters for program offerings that align with the mission. The director of the library or the director of programming for the library usually writes the guidelines. These guidelines often align with your library's or organization's strategic plan and can be rewritten each year. The person writing the guidelines will think of the library's five- or ten-year goals and use those to inform the parameters they set. These parameters are not meant to be restrictive. Instead, they are intended to maximize the efficaciousness of the library's staff time and budgets by focusing on the areas where they can be most impactful.

The programming guidelines will align with the library's mission statement. For example, in Charlotte, North Carolina, the mission statement is to "improve lives and build a stronger community." Therefore, the programming guidelines include the following focal points:

- Literacy and Educational Success improves lives through the gain of literacy and critical-thinking skills; strengthens the community through higher rates of educational success.
- Community Conversations improves lives by encouraging positive dialogue among disparate social groups; strengthens the community by providing public forums where ideas can be shared, discussed, and built upon.
- College and Career Development improves lives by providing introductions to skills and resources necessary for library customers to gain fulfilling employment; strengthens the community by preparing citizens for career opportunities in their area.
- Continual Learning for Adults improves lives by providing continuing education for adults and enhanced quality of life; strengthens the community by enhancing the quality of life for adults in the area.
- Welcome CLT improves lives by providing citizenship instruction and welcoming new residents; strengthens the community by providing a smooth transition to people moving into the city.

In addition to aligning with the library's mission statement, these programming guidelines also line up with Charlotte Mecklenburg Library's vision for how to best impact their community. For example, Charlotte was identified as a community struggling to advance their citizens into careers. The library responded by emphasizing college and career development programs to give residents a better chance of fulfilling employment. Programming guidelines of any kind will help library staff make sure they offer engaging services for their customers while making the most significant possible impact through unified goals.

TYING YOUR PROGRAMS TO YOUR MISSION STATEMENT

The example mission statements included in this chapter's opening focus on offering products, programs, and services that will improve their customers' lives, bring together diverse populations, and strengthen the community. Beyond that, you will also need to make sure that your technology purchases and programs align with your programming guidelines. While some libraries have a broad range of discretion in developing programs for teens, other libraries may have strict parameters or budgets within which to work. Individual missions may vary slightly, but aiming to improve lives, bring together diverse populations, and strengthen communities will always be a good idea.

TECHNOLOGY PROGRAMS THAT IMPROVE LIVES

When thinking of improving teens' lives, one of the first things to come to mind is improving their present circumstances. Teens are experiencing accelerated mental and physical growth and can use all the support that we can offer for success at school, at work, and in the community. Technology programs provide a firm foundation for accomplishing all of these.

Throughout the entire year, teens receive educational support from their local library. This support can be traditional homework and research assistance during the school term, but it can also be through programs. Programs can be both engaging and informative, and sometimes they can teach without the teen participants even realizing it. In the summer, fun programs can teach skills and keep brains limber while preventing the summer slide. Technology programs are well poised to fill this role. At a library branch in Charlotte,

North Carolina, teen-serving staff facilitated a program during the school year that challenged teens to program a Sphero robot to complete a masking-taped maze on the floor successfully. The teens learned a form of coding, learned teamwork, and kept their brains limber.

Additionally, programs such as presentations by professionals in technology fields can help support teens' entry into careers. Teens are poised to transition from school into further education or jobs, and library staff can assist through the offering of programs that introduce teens to their post–high school options. Chances to interact with adults in the community who already have successful careers in technology fields are exciting to teens. They get the opportunity to see the product of their hard work, learn the steps necessary to join that field themselves, and meet a potential mentor. In Charlotte Mecklenburg's ImaginOn branch, a local professional digital photographer came to talk to teens. During the program, one teen, in particular, became slightly more engaged than others and had many questions at the end. By the time the photographer ended the program, he had allowed the teen to try out his digital photography equipment and exchanged contact information if the teen was available and interested in a potential summer internship. Without library programs such as this one, the teen may not have discovered an interest in digital photography or had the opportunity to connect with a potential mentor and kick-start his career.

Furthermore, teens gain vocational experience by interning or volunteering at their local library to lead library programs. Nationwide, teens have seen success after adding "internship facilitating technology programs at local library" to their resumes. Teen-serving library staff provide invaluable training in job readiness, interviewing, workplace interactions, and customer-service skills. Libraries with makerspaces can create internships or volunteer opportunities for teens. From the start, this can provide job readiness experience: the librarians can take the time to craft a job description and ask interested teens to submit applications. Teens gain practice tailoring an application to job qualifications.

Furthermore, instituting an interview process allows teens to speak with professionals about a position and receive feedback in a safe environment. Once a teen has accepted an internship or volunteer position, they begin the experience of receiving instruction from a superior, gain communication skills for the workplace and with customers, and build commitment to a role. While teens provide a service to your library when facilitating technology programs or experiences in your space, you are, in turn, providing the teens with job readiness training.

Among the many ways to improve teens' lives, helping them prepare for success in life, at school, and in a potential career will never be a waste of time. Whether you are the one facilitating the program in which they are introduced to new technology or professions, or they are facilitating the program and learning job readiness skills, you are sure to be improving their lives.

TECHNOLOGY PROGRAMS TO BRING TOGETHER DIVERSE POPULATIONS

Every day, it becomes ever more essential to create spaces where diverse community members can come together and interact. Libraries are perfectly poised to fulfill this role. There already are places where people of all ages, races, and national origins come together; the next step is to connect those diverse populations within your library programs. When this happens, connections are formed, which leads to higher social capital for participants and stronger social infrastructure for the community.

Figure 4.1. Teen volunteer assists with technology program. *Photo by Marie Harris*

Teens can easily develop social capital within technology-based programs. First, let us define social capital. *Social capital* refers to connections between people that positively affect the individuals' ability to achieve success. Often, this is seen in the employment search. You may have heard it said that "it's not what you know, but who you know" when looking for a job. This refers to when someone seems to rise unusually fast in their career and may also have personal connections with upper management. In this case, it may appear that who the person knows is a better indicator of success than what the person knows. Having a broad social network is another part of social capital and can play a positive role in determining whether a person can easily locate housing or employment. Think of how often you may have found a good deal on an item, secured a nice apartment, or landed an interview based on a tip from an acquaintance. Unfortunately, some portions of the population may be at a disadvantage for building social capital. Those who have grown up in or currently live in lower socioeconomic conditions, for example, are usually at risk for having little social capital. Libraries can be places where people across socioeconomic bands, cultural lines, and generations come together in a program and strengthen their social capital.

Technology programs that bring together teens from varying socioeconomic bands or cultural groups allow teens to interact with and know those who are not like themselves. It has been said that libraries should aim for collections that provide both "mirrors" and "windows" for the people they serve. This means that the items should reflect the customer's personal experiences and provide insight into others' lives. Our programs should aim to serve the same purpose. When we offer teens programs, we do not set parameters around them that would exclude teens based on the ability to pay or on nationality. A program based out of Boulder, Colorado, brings together nondisabled teens to develop tactile picture books for children who are blind, and the books often include embedded electronic triggers. The developers in Boulder train library staff from across the country in the administration of this program. When replicated in Charlotte, North Carolina, the inaugural group of teen participants represented various nationalities. Throughout the weeklong program, they formed bonds and shared information about visits to family in other countries or cultural behaviors that might differ from others' experiences. By the program's conclusion, they had developed tactile picture books and skills with programming electronic sensors and formed relationships with teens they may never have met otherwise. They shared social media usernames and cell phone numbers and expanded their potential social capital over a technology-inclusive program.

Technology can also bring people together across generations. Penn State University worked with Generations United to develop a guidebook to intergenerational programs utilizing technology after recognizing a pattern of offerings across the nation. One of the shared highlights in the report is that "the use of technology provides the opportunity for our various age groups to bond together in a common interest."[7] Furthermore, the guidebook references the "EU Kids Online Final Report" that found that only 36 percent of youth ages nine to sixteen thought it was "very true" that they knew more about the internet than their parents.[8] "Digital citizenship" is no longer a given among youth. Technology-based programs can go both ways: They can consist of youth teaching older adults about privacy concerns or fake news, or they can be formed around older adults teaching youth about specific software. One digital area where teens excel is social media. Teens are well poised to assist older adults in entering and interacting on social media platforms. Many teens have been using platforms such as Facebook since their preteen years. They can help older adults create accounts, navigate the social media sphere, and connect with their loved ones. In return, older adults can teach specific software programs to teens. In chapter 11, you will find a full outline for starting a Technology Tutoring program to bring together diverse generations. If your library has a makerspace, a professional engineer could facilitate a program to teach young adults how to utilize a computer-aided drafting program and then 3D print their creations. Beyond instruction, entertaining technology programs can also bring together generations. One teen librarian offers frequent "retro gaming" programs. During these programs, teens and older adults come together to experience early video games. The librarian regularly observes older adults giving the teenaged patrons combinations and hints to beat the games.[9]

Social infrastructure is a fantastic result of both types of programs. In *Palaces for the People*, Eric Klinenberg writes about how genuinely open and public places such as libraries can be indicators for the health of the community.[10] When people of different socioeconomic status, nationality, and age come together to learn and share, connections are made that strengthen the whole community. Klinenberg researched a 1995 heat wave in Chicago that had a devastating death toll. He found that higher socioeconomic areas did well and found that lower socioeconomic areas with strong social infrastructure also fared well. He found that when a community had strong interpersonal connections, people were more likely to bond together and assist one another, leading to an increased survival rate in the face of a natural disaster. He revisited this research in 2018 in preparation for writing *Palaces for the People* and found that public spaces such as libraries continue to contribute to strong social infrastructure today.[11]

To this end, the public library in Beaverton, Oregon, takes technology such as Ozobots, Dashes, and Code-a-Pillars with them to outreach programs in the city's parks.[12] In this way, the library meets the people where they are. Outreach programs are a great way to build social infrastructure as they organically bring together people from varying socioeconomic and generational groups into a neutral space.

TECHNOLOGY PROGRAMS THAT BUILD A STRONGER COMMUNITY

Technology-based programs can align with your library's mission in the building of a stronger community. As mentioned, author Klinenberg was able to identify a correlation between public libraries and resilient communities. He saw libraries offering programs that connected people. When people feel connected within their community, they are more likely to take care of the neighborhood and one another.

Programs that utilize technology can strengthen a community. Some segments of a city may be able to afford digital devices in their homes, but other segments may not. Providing access to these devices during library programs allows the less fortunate to interact with machines necessary for life in our modern society. Many libraries now have devices available for checkout or use at a technology bar. With many schools now requiring students to complete or turn in assignments electronically, having access to computers and other devices is of utmost importance. One way in which a library can help provide this access is through device bars or computer labs. Furthermore, the library may decide to staff the space with employees or volunteers who can assist teens unfamiliar with the devices.

Additionally, reflect on technology programs that bring together diverse populations. These programs certainly help to build a stronger community. The programs do not have to be restricted to different generations teaching each other new skills, either. The programs could also bring together attendees to learn about new technology. A library in Greenville County, South Carolina, offered a program at which participants ages thirteen and older had the opportunity to hear from an astronomer about the Apollo moon landing. This free library program brought together people of all ages and walks of life to learn more about space exploration technology. Another type of library program that would strengthen the community would be one in which teens learn leadership and workplace skills. Many teen librarians work with young adults one on one or in small groups to train them in working with older adults or with young children in technology-rich environments such as a makerspace or studio. In these programs, teens get to share their enthusiasm for tech with others and learn how to comport themselves in the workplace. One final program idea would be to institute a technology-based book club wherein teens from every background can discuss articles or books that address issues with or new ideas from the technology sphere.

When interacting with others outside of their usual social sphere, teens can become part of a more tightly woven community fabric. In intergenerational programs, they learn empathy and patience and the value of shared ideas. In leadership or volunteer roles, they learn self-motivation, teaching, communication, and workplace expectations. In technology-based book clubs, teens can learn communication and understanding of others' backgrounds. As discussed previously, tight-knit communities are better able to maintain positive growth.

CONCLUSION

Teens, technology, and library spaces are a guarantee for success, so long as the programs that provide those elements align with your library's mission. Keep in mind the library's vision and programming guidelines, and be prepared to see teens make great strides in improving their own lives and the lives of those around them. With many mission statements generally applying to improving lives, bringing together diverse populations, and building a stronger community, it becomes clear why it is important to stick to these goals and not merely buy into fad technology.

Teens can get involved with technology in their library in innumerable ways while contributing to the mission's success. First, they can enjoy programs in which they meet professionals in technology fields, learn new software or programming skills in a group setting, or participate in a tech-themed book club. Second, they can fully participate in other programs' success, such as information sharing across generations, volunteer work at a library technology program, or an internship in a library makerspace or studio. No matter the level of involvement, teens will be learning critical skills for working together across socioeconomic levels and generations and contributing to the strength of their community's social fabric.

Library mission statements are foundational to library services. They help to guide what programs and services are offered to use library funds and staff most efficaciously. Mission statements should always be considered, alongside vision statements and programming guidelines (if applicable), when planning your technology-based programs for teens.

NOTES

1. "About." Charlotte Mecklenburg Library (NC). Accessed June 21, 2019. https://cmlibrary.org/about.
2. "Mission and Strategic Plan." Beaverton City Library (OR). Accessed August 13, 2019. https://www.beavertonlibrary.org/323/Mission—Strategic—Plan.
3. "About CCPL." Charleston County Public Library (SC). Accessed June 21, 2019. https://www.ccpl.org/about.
4. "Cleveland Public Library." Cleveland Public Library (OH). Accessed June 21, 2019. https://cpl.org/.
5. "About Us." Greenville County Library System (SC). Accessed July 8, 2019. https://www.greenvillelibrary.org/about-us.
6. Nous, Rebecca. "Building Cathedrals: Mission Statements in Academic Libraries." *Library Leadership & Management (Online)*, 29, no. 4 (2015): 1–12. http://nclive.org/cgi—bin/nclsm?url=http://search.proquest.com/docview/1707792538?accountid=13217.
7. Kaplan, Matthew, Mariano Sánchez, Cecil Shelton, and Leah Bradley. *Using Technology to Connect Generations*. University Park, PA: Penn State University and Washington, DC, 2013. http://extension.psu.edu/youth/intergenerational/program-areas/technology.
8. Kaplan, Sánchez, Shelton, and Bradley. *Using Technology to Connect Generations*.
9. Personal communication. Kaitlyn Gundlach. October 21, 2019.
10. Klinenberg, Eric. *Palaces for the People: How Social Infrastructure Can Help Fight Inequality, Polarization, and the Decline of Civic Life*. New York: Crown, 2018.
11. Klinenberg. *Palaces for the People*.
12. Wyckoff, Amy. "Technology + Teens + Vocational Readiness." Email. 2019.

Part II

Connecting Teens with Technology

FIVE

Mentorship

*I **love** what I do and my team. They make the magic happen, and I get excited when they grow up and out (even though the loss is great)! Mentorship and developing people bring me deep satisfaction.*

—Gretchen Caserotti[1]

MENTORSHIP

This chapter looks at different ways that guidance can be provided for the community and within the library profession and how library staff can create opportunities for mentoring youth focused on technology. We bring some new constructs of what mentoring can look like, mainly through an equity, diversity, and inclusion lens. When we are aware of the power and privilege we may have, then we can create less harm to one another.

Let us start with some exploration into what mentorship can look like within the profession or, in other words, paired with someone else in a similar job experience. We look at why mentorship can be useful, especially regarding technology that changes so quickly. Chances are what you learned in library school already became dated by the time you started your new job. As a result of processes changing within your library system, such as a new online catalog or a grant that can purchase new technology gadgets, you will likely even be forced to learn how to use something you didn't know how to use before. You will want to be familiar with how you approach learning when a new initiative is given to you or decide if you will develop the leading action yourself. Do you tend to put it off if you can or automatically reach out and start putting minds together to figure out how something works? Determining how you approach learning can help decide the kind of mentor you want or want to be. There is no right or wrong answer here. Get rid of the limiting beliefs you might have for yourself in that you are not tech-savvy or are a technophobe. It is okay to learn how to do something and not catch on as fast as another person. Pairing up with someone in the profession might be just the thing to jump-start your way to teaching someone else! Setting aside intentional time by noting it on your calendar and breaking down goals into smaller steps are a few ways to get started and reach the end goal in a way that feels less intimidating. You can also work backward from a "soft" scheduled pilot program where the bar to "failing" is low or nonexistent. For example, if you plan on learning how to integrate new robots into an upcoming program, have other gadgets and skilled navigators available. If something does not work, there is less pressure to fix it right then and there, and you can move onto something that you have done before and is more guaranteed to work. Besides, most teens are up for a good challenge and welcome the opportunity to step up and show their knowledge on how to get something working.

Your library location may not provide formal mentorship or technology-learning opportunities as part of your orientation or ongoing professional development. Perhaps your supervisor is the de facto mentor, or you strike up a bond with one of your co-workers who seems to be the designated technology guru, and they take you under their wing. Both are opportunities that you can learn from, so do not quickly dismiss the exchange of information that may be given even if you are looking for something different. But also know the value in a formal mentor relationship that you may need to search for outside of your department, branch, division, or even system.

MENTORING OPPORTUNITIES WITH ALA

Many ALA divisions, round tables, and affiliates have a mentoring program for members. The earliest press release found online for YALSA's program was in 2010. It involved an application process and mutual guidance and support for both the "experienced librarian" of six or more years and the protégé who was beginning their library experience "to provide the best services possible to teens in their local communities."[2] As of 2017, an update to the program was proposed due in part to a declining number of applications and wanting to "align it more with YALSA's new goals and priorities," according to a YALSA Board document and blog post.[3] One suggestion was to offer both short- and long-term opportunities on an "as-needed" basis to accommodate people's schedules. As of this writing, the launch was proposed for March 2020, but due to COVID, it was temporarily delayed.[4]

Keep checking back with YALSA to see the next iteration of formal mentoring. Do not discount opportunities to join a jury, task force, or committee where you can inadvertently still gain skills and knowledge as an informal opportunity. While you might not opt to be the chair of a group until you achieve a bit more experience, learning how to work with other members across the nation in a shared endeavor will undoubtedly help build more scaffolding to your already existing foundation.

Also, do not be afraid to check out opportunities through other divisions, round tables, and affiliates with ALA. There is an entire page on ALA's site dedicated to mentoring resources.[5]

Check out your state library opportunities as well. Most states have a Youth Services Consultant and, of course, a web presence as a starting point. If nothing obvious exists, reach out to them directly and see if you can start something formal yourself.

Additionally, be on the lookout for informal circumstances such as a workshop you may attend with a cohort. One of my closest professional relationships began with someone who gave a conference presentation on a programming topic for which I was enthusiastic. After the conference, I reached out to them about a controversial comment they made that I agreed with, and we have worked together informally in various ways ever since!

Do not discount occasions outside of the library profession for mentorship opportunities. If you are looking to make leadership strides, a career coach may have that perspective. Sure, they may cost money, and we do not want to break the bank over this, but perhaps a small or short-term investment might get you where you want to be. They may even be able to share some free resources that you had not thought of before if you are not in a particularly financially healthy place. Even just polishing up a resume or social media site while you are not actively looking can give you some momentum to gather content at a more relaxed pace instead of when you're frantically job searching or unemployed. Visiting LinkedIn (http://www.linkedIn.com) or searching for career coaches in your area can be a great start. My city and state are among several locations that offer online workshops through SkillPop (http://www.skillpop.com), where I found my current coach. While that class did meet in person, there is also SkillPop Anywhere that offers classes to learn online from home. Fees generally range from $15 to $40 for a wide variety of classes. There are many classes that concentrate on developing leadership skills, understanding the self better through the Enneagram, and updating or starting your LinkedIn page (or the equivalent of a professional social networking site at the time of this reading). If SkillPop is not accessible, the closest parallel may be a class at your community college or some form of continuing education for adults.

MENTORING THE COMMUNITY

As of this writing, while the pandemic certainly caused (and continues to cause) an unprecedented number of job losses, some people were able to reinvent themselves. They became entrepreneurs based on a skill they wanted to cultivate. As a result, there is a rise in coaches willing to provide their expertise on using social media to grow a business or start one. For example, many libraries remained closed during the beginning of the pandemic in early 2020. If they wanted to continue to stay relevant to the public, they would need to pivot many of their services. In April 2020, the Public Library Association (PLA) distributed a survey that garnered around 2,500 responses, according to an ALA press release. Close to 98 percent of people who replied did note the close of their buildings, but virtual storytimes, library cards, or even utilizing the library space for a day shelter were not uncommon endeavors at the time.[6] According to *Insider*, "access to public space has been restricted in the pandemic, from libraries to parks to transit to sidewalks."[7] The closures disproportionately affected the most vulnerable, such as those in rural areas, persons experiencing homelessness, and disabled people. The reason closures and access are mentioned in this chapter is because the issue exposes the needs that still exist in communities that organizations may not be able to fill. Grassroots organizations or even individuals have seen a need to step up and fill a gap. For example, many public libraries' initial phases allowed limited services such as mobile printing, coming in to check out materials on hold, and attending virtual programs. The community center a few blocks away from my branch was offering opportunities for community members to assist youth on the computers to help find jobs or do their homework. This is just one example of the kind of community mentoring that we need to look for opportunities to develop. "Mentoring is an excellent tool for helping people, especially through periods of growth and transitions."[8]

It is also important that we know any biases we may consciously or subconsciously hold toward another that may reveal themselves in any superior/inferior relationship. We want to model respect for one another and be aware of any privileges we carry that we might bring to the interaction. For a more in-depth discussion on the work of inclusivity, one resource is the 2019 report on Social Location from the National Council on Family Relations.[9] For example, actions such as body language may be conveying a whole lot more than we are aware of or even intended—though the impact of our actions is the key to bringing more awareness to our behavior with one another.

Another example of community mentoring is a program at the Cincinnati Public Library, which began offering homework help in September 2020. They are holding student-only hours, limiting the amount of time they can utilize the building resources, and training staff to help families navigate the online space.[10] As mentioned in previous chapters, outreach to the community is a standard part of many public libraries' services, as you likely know from your own library experiences. Offering these services during a pandemic exposes the community's needs that have been there all along. These mentor relationships do not need to stop just because our libraries may be closed temporarily due to safety precautions; they may just look different than we are used to, but we can still find ways to make them happen. You may be surprised who you know and where your passion within the library profession (or otherwise!) may lead. The pandemic allowed many to slow down and think about what was important to them individually. Organizationally, many were able to reassess their position within their communities and make changes based on what the new needs revealed themselves to be.

Mentoring can be messy when trying to find the right match. When looking for an adviser to meet your needs, or when someone wants you to mentor them, figure out what critical needs the community has and what resources are available. Also be aware of what needs to change and the effective role you can play in assisting and leading that change. Keep in mind that what worked with one person may not be the same for another, and as your circumstances and desires change, you may need to find different people to meet your needs as well.

YOUTH MENTORSHIP

We now move on to looking at mentoring teens at the library. The Search Institute is a well-known organization that has developed a Developmental Assets Framework that identifies forty supports and strengths for helping young people succeed. These often-cited measures are shown to shore up youth from experiencing further risk, and they look at mentorship as an asset of support. They state that having "other adult relationships" where a "young person receives support from three or more nonparent adults"[11] is an essential external asset that helps youth to grow up healthy. The Search Institute explains a bit further what support from another adult means in the context of mentorship:

> Sometimes we think of mentors narrowly as those who sign up through a formal program to spend time with a young person. In addition to these formal mentors, informal or everyday mentors can be any trustworthy adult who offers support, guidance, and encouragement to help young people overcome challenges and become their best selves.

They then break it down into five specific actions that show the kind of relationship that can be built for the youth. Adult mentors (1) express care when they genuinely form relationships with youth, (2) challenge growth by encouraging the youth to improve and do their best, (3) provide support by giving feedback and guidance, (4) share power by enabling youth voices at the table, and lastly, (5) expand possibilities by connecting youth to "opportunities for growth and discovery."[12]

The assets above overlap into another structure called Connected Learning. Connected Learning[13] is a framework many libraries use, including YALSA, to bridge the gap between youth and opportunities. The mentorship piece is reflected in the supportive relationships that play a role in helping youth pair their passions and interests with future goals. If you want to take a deeper dive into applying Connected Learning to your library, check out their website. They have a wealth of resources, reports, and examples of how youth show positive results when the framework is applied. You may find some grant-funded courses available through YALSA, or check your state organization to learn how to create engaging teen programs through this model.

In looking at either the Search Institute's Developmental Assets or the Connected Learning framework developed by the Connected Learning Alliance, you can decide how to utilize these mentorship frameworks in your library. If you are looking for something more specifically related to technology, determine the program's format and purpose first and then set about looking to develop partnerships in the community that might be able to lend a hand. If anything, the pandemic has taught us that we are a lot more connected than we might have previously realized. If someone does not have time to meet in person each week or their physical location isn't close, they still might be willing to get online for a Zoom call with a teen wanting some advice on getting started on a different career path.

STUDIO I / MAKERSPACE VOLUNTEERING

Since my library branch opened in the early 2000s, we have had a technology mentor program with a space called Studio i. It was initially designed with a focus on filmmaking. The last five years incorporated more of a makerspace feel with equipment such as a 3D printer and vinyl cutter for youth to experiment with creating what they wanted to. Here, we look at a few of the iterations that the teen mentoring program went through, and some pros and cons. We always approached each incorporation with the attitude of trying to see if it worked, and if it did not, we were flexible and tried something different the next time around.

The volunteer program runs year-round and is an opportunity for teens to learn new technology, show other youth how to use the equipment, and develop additional projects or knowledge about the equipment they have not tried before. Teens assist in this program after school and on weekends during the school year and in various shifts throughout the summer. While we have group visits during the day for homeschoolers or those in school taking a field trip, the demand is not enough to recruit volunteers (people who are likely homeschooled, have an alternative schedule, or are a recent graduate) to help. When the program was in its infancy during the first few years, one staff member oversaw everything from recruitment to the volunteers' day-to-day tasks. Any one person found it difficult to keep up with and give the teens the adequate support they needed, even though we could determine how many volunteers were required per term. Some libraries may not have the staff to do otherwise. Since we did, we assigned a contact—a staff person who could make sure the teen was on track (are they showing up for their shift on time, are they pursuing a project they are interested in, etc.).

One of the main changes we made to the program was to align it with the systemwide volunteer program (called VolunTeen) when applications were considered (three times a year) and when terms started and finished. The terms were loosely in alignment with the school year (fall, spring, and summer). This was an update from a revolving-door scenario where you and the teen were unsure where they stood in the program. The downsides of this approach might mean a teen missed a deadline, or there was a shortage or plethora of applicants one term compared to another. Communication and marketing can help.

Another change that was made with the program was that for so long, the Studio i volunteers were considered a separate program from those who did the shelving or helped with children's programs. The more the technology became part of the way we did daily services, became an integrated part of the library, and was utilized by customers (busier in the summer with groups, for example), the less it made sense to separate. In other words, it was just as important for a volunteer to know how to shelve books as it was for them to learn what the makerspace offered to be able to give an elevator speech to a customer, even if it took them a bit more time to learn the equipment than someone else. We believed that a holistic approach allowed for a more realistic sense of what the library offered and for peer mentoring opportunities among the volunteers when they worked the same shift.

The other change we implemented to the program was the choice to "level up" their experience, especially if they had been there for a prior term. It was not a completely gamified program where they earned badges for performing specific duties, but it created a kind of scaffolding to support them as they moved through the term. For example, if they did not bring experience to the program, they could spend their first few weeks getting acquainted with the various software and hardware by performing basic steps and small projects. Consecutive terms could be spent further developing those projects into a program or tutorial for customers. A sample track is included at the end of the chapter.

This approach was very much youth-led in that they could decide on a focus. The track gave library staff and youth structure in further growing their skills and taking on new challenges. This organization also helped articulate the possibilities instead of feeling like we were being "put on the spot" to develop something that might not appeal to the youth. The tracks also had enough flexibility that if the teen changed their mind and decided for whatever reason they wanted to switch gears and no longer pursue their original project, they were welcome to change course.

Lastly, within this program we seek to help youth articulate what they have learned from volunteering with the library and show them how those skills are valuable within the workforce. While they do not need to pursue a career based on the technology they are learning, they will inevitably apply time management and taking direction no matter what path they decide to follow as they further their education, develop their passion, or find a job. During an exit interview, we talk through what they have learned and if they reached their goals. Hopefully, they want to return for another term if they are a good fit for the program.

VolunTeen Studio i Track: Overview and Resources Sample

Studio i visitors can express themselves through animated and live-action videos, music, or other tools, including graphic design, drawing, and even robotics. Studio i houses a variety of equipment used to create content—whether it is for a school project or a hobby. Such equipment includes the following:

1. iPads and iMacs
2. Blue screen
3. ReadyANIMATOR
4. Recording booth
5. Computers for video and photo editing
6. Sewing machine
7. Silhouette die-cut machine
8. MIDI-enabled keyboard

Some of this equipment has apps and additional components to create more complex projects. Still, it is important first to understand the basic software, as these will be features and applications that most visitors to Studio i will seek to experience. These include the following:

1. Veescope Live
2. iMovie
3. Stop Motion Studio
4. GarageBand

Levels and Evaluation

Proficiency in Studio i software will be determined by the completion of a level-appropriate task or project. VolunTeens looking to further their skills in Studio i may continue to the Intermediate and Advanced levels of the Studio i track. The parameters for the levels given to the teens are as follows:

Basic

1. Complete all Basic Learning Objectives.
2. Demonstrate/explain two new things you learned about any of the Studio i equipment/software.

Intermediate

1. Complete all Intermediate Learning Objectives.

Choose one:

1. Complete a self-directed project using Studio i equipment and software. Examples of projects include stop-motion animation short films, iMovie trailers, GarageBand instrumentals, etc.
2. Create a how-to guide for a piece of Studio i equipment or software. How-to guides may be presented as a video, flow-chart, pamphlet, etc.

Advanced

1. Complete all Advanced Learning Objectives.

Choose one:

1. Complete a self-directed project using a combination of two or more pieces of Studio i equipment and software. For example, create a short film using both the blue screen and stop-motion animation.
2. Develop and facilitate a teen or pre-teen program highlighting Studio i equipment and software.

Personal Goals

1. Consider your own goals as you learn about Studio i and work on projects. What are the three skills you want to develop or things you want to learn during this term?

Learning Resources

VolunTeens are expected to be able to demonstrate proficiency with Studio i equipment and software. In addition to hands-on learning and built-in tutorials, VolunTeens have a collection of online resources at their disposal to aid in learning and proficiency.

Many of these online resources originate from Lynda.com, an online educational site with more than 3,000 courses available to Charlotte Mecklenburg Library cardholders for free. Lynda.com must be accessed through the library's online portal: https://www.lynda.com/portal/sip?org=cmlibrary.org. The Lynda login for VolunTeens is as follows:

> Library card number:
> Password:
> Click on the username in the top right corner, then select the playlist entitled Studio i Essential Training for VolunTeens to find the recommended videos for beginners. For

VolunTeens ready to move onto projects, the playlist Studio i Project Creation is available for training.

For information on learning resources for the equipment and software used at Studio i, check out the following sources and see what may work for you as you develop new teen technology programs in your libraries:

Video Creation: Veescope Live (iPad only), iMovie
Available on iPad and Mac

1. Lynda.com: iMovie 10.1.1 Essential Training (Studio i Essential Training playlist)
2. Apple Support—iMovie Help for iPad: https://help.apple.com/imovie/ipad
3. Apple Support—iMovie Help for Mac: https://help.apple.com/imovie/mac

Stop Motion Animation: ReadyANIMATOR (device), I Can Animate, Stop Motion Studio
Available on iPad and iPod Touch

1. Lynda.com: Learning Stop Motion Animation (Studio i Essential Training playlist)
2. ReadyANIMATOR: https://www.readyanimator.com/how-to/
3. I Can Animate: http://www.kudlian.net/products/icananimatev2/tutorials.html
4. Stop Motion Studio: http://bit.ly/stopmotionsupport

Sound Booth: GarageBand
Available on iPad and Mac

1. Lynda.com: GarageBand '09 Essential Training (Studio i Essential Training playlist)
2. GarageBand '09—Getting Started Manual: http://apple.co/2kosQxd

Sewing Machine

1. Dwell on Joy—Sewing Machine 101: http://bit.ly/2r675Uu
2. Instructables.com—Sewing 101 Collection (You → Draft Collections or Favorites)

NOTES

1. Caserotti, Gretchen (@gcaserotti). Twitter. September 21, 2020. https://twitter.com/gcaserotti/status/1308242187583275009.
2. "YALSA Launches Mentoring Program." ALA News and Press Center. March 16, 2010. http://www.ala.org/news/news/pressreleases2010/march2010/mentor_yalsa.
3. YALS Editorial Advisory Board. "YALS 2017 Summer Resources: Learning from Each Other: Successful Mentoring/Protege Relationships." YALSA Blog. July 10, 2017. http://yalsa.ala.org/blog/2017/07/10/yals-2017-summer-resources-learning-from-each-other-successful-mentoringprotege-relationships/.
4. "YALSA's Virtual Mentoring Program." Young Adult Library Services Association (YALSA). Accessed September 28, 2020. http://www.ala.org/yalsa/profdev/mentoring.
5. "ALA Mentoring Resources." ALA Education and Careers. November 3, 2017. http://www.ala.org/educationcareers/mentoring/mentoring_and_recruitment_efforts.
6. Morales, Macey, and Shawnda Hines. "Public Libraries Launch, Expand Services during COVID-19 Pandemic." ALA News and Press Center. April 9, 2020. http://www.ala.org/news/press-releases/2020/04/public-libraries-launch-expand-services-during-covid-19-pandemic-0.
7. Haigney, Sophie. "The Pandemic Is Transforming How Americans Use Public Libraries, Parks, and Streets—and It's Depriving Vulnerable People of Space When They Need It Most." *Insider*. September 14, 2020. https://www.insider.com/how-public-space-will-change-after-pandemic-class-race-inequality-2020-9.
8. Dodge, Kathryn E. "Community Mentoring: A Tool for Successful Communities." *Journal of Extension (JOE)*, 53, no. 1 (2015). Accessed September 29, 2020. https://www.joe.org/joe/2015february/iw2.php.

9. "Inclusion and Diversity Committee Report: What's Your Social Location?" National Council on Family Relations. Accessed September 29, 2020. https://www.ncfr.org/ncfr-report/spring-2019/inclusion-and-diversity-social-location.

10. Parrish, Morgan. "Cincinnati Public Library of Hamilton County Launches New Program to Help CPS Kids with Remote Learning." https://www.fox19.com. August 22, 2020. https://www.fox19.com/2020/08/22/cincinnati-public-library-hamilton-county-launches-new-program-help-cps-kids-with-remote-learning/.

11. "The Developmental Assets Framework." Search Institute. November 5, 2019. https://www.search-institute.org/our-research/development-assets/developmental-assets-framework/.

12. "What Do Mentors Do That Matters?" Search Institute. January 4, 2016. http://www.search-institute.org/what-do-mentors-do-that-matters.

13. "About Connected Learning." Connected Learning Alliance. October 12, 2018. https://clalliance.org/about-connected-learning/.

SIX
Career Readiness and Exploration

Many libraries across the country focus on career readiness in their teen programming, at least in a small part. Libraries have diverse reasons behind their decision to focus on this topic. One common reason libraries provide these programs is in reaction to the reality that their communities lack the technical knowledge needed for the jobs moving into the area. Numerous articles and reports speak of this gap between local citizens' technological skills and the required employment experience by companies moving into the area.

In Charlotte, the Charlotte Mecklenburg Library made career and college readiness one of their key program focuses for teens following a report by Harvard and UC Berkeley in 2013 that named the city the worst (of fifty chosen for the study) for the economic advancement of its citizens.[1] In response to this study, the city convened a Leading on Opportunity Task Force to develop strategies for improving Charlotte's standing. One of the areas identified as a method for improving Charlotteans' economic advancement opportunity was college and career readiness. Some of the specific recommendations included the following:

- "Students need to be prepared for our rapidly-changing workforce needs. A rapidly-changing job market has opened other pathways to equip our students with the skills and education they will need to build and support thriving families."
- "Broaden the range of and access to high-quality college and career pathways offered by our K–12 and postsecondary institutions, ensuring all students have access to and support for the full range of opportunities."
- "Create more on-ramps to education, training, and employment for our disconnected youth and young adults."[2]

Charlotte is not alone in this endeavor. Many cities, especially in the southern United States, struggle to provide their citizens with the necessary preparation for available employment. The South has been a desired geographic location for businesses and corporations for many decades. Property costs and taxes tend to be lower, fair weather prevails for much of the year, and lower cost of living means that salaries for employees are lower. These businesses often arrive in southern cities with their employees or attract out-of-state talent. Local residents are not usually equipped for more technical or advanced positions within the company.

Birmingham, Alabama, is an example of this. Once known as the "Pittsburgh of the South" for its robust manufacturing industry, it is now reimagining itself as the "Silicon Valley of the South" with a growing number of technological corporations setting up offices. However, many Birmingham residents lack the digital skills necessary to cross over from more manual careers to the new technology-related positions. The public library can step in and help improve lives and build a stronger community.

The library offers everything from basic computer classes to experiences in digital makerspace studios in Birmingham. These free programs allow community members to gain the skills necessary to advance in employment. The Birmingham system and other public libraries in similar situations were featured in an article in *The Atlantic*. In one example, a Birmingham resident was ready to advance into a supervisory role in the service industry, but she lacked the technological knowledge to manage schedules and timesheets online. Her new employer suggested the library, where she found classes that prepared her to step into her new role and succeed. In another example, a librarian at a Cuyahoga County Public Library branch in Ohio helped a patron create their first email address to complete an online job application.[3]

Libraries are well poised to meet this need for technology instruction even before a patron enters the workforce for the first time. While the patrons described in the article from *The Atlantic* were adults changing careers that a library could help, teens can also benefit from technology training or introduction. They are just entering the workforce, but even entry-level jobs require a basic familiarity with computers. McDonald's restaurants have computerized ordering stations and electronic cash registers. Supermarket stockers carry handheld scanners to keep track of inventory on the shelves. Even babysitters may now use cell phones to send pictures and updates to parents. Library programs can help introduce teens to the technology they will be using as they enter the workforce and experiment with it before using it in the workplace.

Libraries provide teens fail-safe places to experiment with technology. Libraries can also offer spaces for teens to explore career options without commitment. Teens can try their hand at "employment" (often volunteer work or internships) without risk. They can apply for, interview for, and then work in library jobs in makerspaces short-term. If they do not enjoy the work, their term will end, and they can move on to exploring other options. Alternatively, teens can attend library programs that allow them to meet and interact with professionals in various technology-related careers. From the comfort of their familiar local library, they can ask these professionals questions about the pathway to their careers and any challenges they may face if they choose to pursue those jobs. Teens' programs can look like formal technology training, informal or fun technology experiences, or work experiences in technology-rich environments, all provided in their local public library.

VOCATIONAL READINESS THROUGH TECHNOLOGY INSTRUCTION

The trustees of what is believed to be the first public library in America, the Boston Public Library, wrote in their very first report to the City of Boston in 1852:

> If the young machinist, engineer, architect, chemist, engraver, painter, instrument-maker, musician (or student of any branch of science or literature) wishes to consult a valuable and especially a rare and costly work, he must buy it, often import it at an expense he can ill afford, or he must be indebted for its use to the liberality of private corporations or individuals. The trustees submit, that for all the reasons for which exist for furnishing the means of elementary education, at the public expense, apply in an equal degree to a reasonable provision to aid and encourage the acquisition of the knowledge required to complete a preparation for active life or to perform its duties.[4]

With these lines in the report, the trustees defined that public libraries are for the people and their further education. When the report was written, this was restricted to a specific group of people, and those people were only able to read books to gain more information. Much later, many libraries added typewriters as a means of helping patrons fulfill their goals. Now, public libraries are open to all, and there are many different ways users can access and gain information, including digitally. Library services go beyond providing print materials for patrons and often provide access to technology and other digital tools and instruction. Through this instruction, teens receive an introduction to technology or access to technology that they may not otherwise experience.

Despite being considered "digital citizens," teens often need formal instruction to fully maximize and take advantage of all that is offered electronically. While they may frame a better social media photo and know the most popular hashtags each day, they may not select the best keywords for a search in an electronic research database. Teen-serving school and public library staff can step in to help. Merely providing access to technology is not enough; it must be coupled with instruction to be used most effectively.

The Organisation for Economic Co-operation and Development completed a study of forty-two countries of varying economic status. They discovered that when teenagers have equal access to the internet, they use it differently depending on their socioeconomic status. Teenagers with greater wealth in their families tended to spend more time reading the news and researching topics of personal and academic interest on the internet. In contrast, those with lesser financial resources tended to spend their time on the internet viewing videos or playing games. Their bottom-line recommendation is to do everything possible to reduce the gap in access and the gap in understanding this resource.[5] Without a solid knowledge of the digital tools at their fingertips, teens are at risk of being unprepared for future employment opportunities.

Digital literacy instruction for teens is important and must be engaging and enjoyable or they will tune out. It is hard to imagine teens willingly attending a library program where they are sitting in orderly rows in a computer lab, diligently learning the basics of Microsoft Word. Easier to picture is a group of teens actively involved in problem-solving or laughing aloud at a fun activity. Some essential skills that you might consider teaching to your teen patrons to prepare them for the workforce include practicing internet privacy, discerning between reliable and unreliable news sources, and using electronic databases.

Internet privacy becomes an increasingly important topic each year. There are hundreds of online articles dedicated to the problem. In 2018, much of the world anxiously watched the trial of Mark Zuckerberg of Facebook, Inc., after accusations of privacy invasion. The company was accused of collecting users' personal information and preferences and then using it to sell targeted advertising. During that trial, people learned that while Facebook, Inc., had included ways users could opt out of publicly sharing their information, those ways were hidden and not intuitive for users to find. Claire Fontaine of the Data & Society Institute conducted a study in 2018 that showed that teens were often well aware of the risks inherent in social media use, but they were also overwhelmed at the level of responsibility that they were forced to take on to protect themselves. One study member said that it was "like getting a tattoo" every time they got online. Fontaine reflected that "a twelve-year-old shouldn't have to present herself as an employable white-collar worker." She recommends that educators work with students to understand and navigate the World Wide Web and protect their privacy. The alternative is that students are forced to become reactive, trying to quickly "clean up" their social media accounts as they approach college or employment applications.[6]

The next step is to develop a method for teaching internet privacy best practices to a group of patrons who want to dive right into the various social media platforms. These programs can be highly engaging and have a tremendous impact. For example, the nonprofit I AM not the MEdia offers workshops for teens that invite them to look closely at the personal "brand" they are developing via social media, how the messages they are consuming online could affect their mental health, and many other workshop choices. The organization brings its workshops to Charlotte, North Carolina, and sells their curriculum online to those who are farther away.[7] Their workshops incorporate current social media platforms and accounts, student use of social media, and supporting media types. Libraries could put on similar programs, even if they could not afford the curriculum package or workshop fee. "Build Your Personal Brand on Social Media" as a program title may be more appealing to teen patrons than "Social Media Privacy Workshop." No matter how these programs are packaged, teen librarians can perform excellent services for teens by emphasizing the importance of protecting their privacy and information online. It could make a big difference in their later employment searches.

Related to social media is the need to teach teens how to discern "real" news or information from "fake" news online. This digital literacy skill will prepare teens for research should they pursue a vocational or collegiate education beyond high school or prepare them to be well-informed citizens as they enter the workforce. It can also directly impact employment in some ways. One library in Charlotte, North Carolina, saw a large influx of people on a Saturday morning after a misleading advertisement for Amazon employment was circulated via Facebook. A quick inspection by library staff revealed that it was created as a hoax or misdirection, but the respondents could not see that. There are many aspects of digital literacy that lifelong users of technology and the internet can pick up on instinctually that must be taught to those new to these experiences. Being able to discern valid sources from those intended to mislead will also help teens avoid being taken advantage of, like the would-be Amazon employees.

Further, predators online will actively con young people out of money or lure them into unsafe situations. While this is a serious outcome, teen librarians could still use gaming to shed light on the topic. Websites such as Quizlet and Kahoot! allow instructors to create game show–style quizzes that students participate in using their (or their library's) mobile devices.

A game can be created for participants to guess which of a set of profiles is a real person versus a fake profile. There could be true or false questions to help teens identify what information (if any) should be given out online and to which sources. Should they give their full name to a person online they have never met in person? Should they use the same password at Target.com that they use for Facebook.com? Should they give the name of their school to an organization or business online? The correct answers can be expanded upon as the game is reviewed. Beyond teaching how to spot what is trustworthy or not on social media, teens will also benefit from learning to discern untrustworthy websites for information.

To engage teens and spark laughter, ask the program attendees to search for information on the Great Pacific Northwest Tree Octopus. The top search results in many popular search engines will be seemingly legitimate websites documenting this fictional creature's biology and recent sightings. When the links are selected, the sites are full of information. All the embedded links work. The website can teach how to spot a nonlegitimate news source, as it also contains plenty of red flags for research, such as a .net address and a lack of supporting documentation in other sources. The humor of picturing a terrestrial octopus is a bonus to the exercise. Instruction in online safety and privacy, whether offered in a fun game or a humorous exercise, is vital to teens' progress to higher education or employment.

Once the teen librarian has revealed that the Great Pacific Northwest Tree Octopus is not a real creature, instruction can begin using reliable sources of information online, such as research databases. A quick search of any reputable electronic database reveals either a complete lack of mention of the octopus or papers referencing the hoax's history and its use in digital literacy instruction. Further, this instruction can have immediate relevance to teens as they work on research assignments or large senior projects. Direct relevance is almost always appealing to teens. Most libraries offer a selection of research databases for their patrons to use. Most patrons, however, are untrained in how to use them. Popular search engines have become incredibly intuitive for users. At Google.com, for example, users can type out their entire question in a full sentence and receive relevant results. Databases, however, ask a bit more of the user. They ask that a type of search (keyword, subject, author, etc.) is selected, and then Boolean entries are filled in. Having had the advantage of more user-friendly online search engines for their entire lives, teens are at a disadvantage with these databases. Even while recognizing that "research database navigation" might not be the most popular program topic to teens, rather than attempting to make it overly playful or lighthearted, focus on the teens to whom the library is marketing the program. It may not be easy to get individual teens or their parents excited about this topic, even when appealing to its relevancy. Instead, offer this program to established groups. Research database navigation can be an appealing offer to school and after-school groups, both in the library and outreach. Teen librarians can set up the program as a requestable group visit for local schools or reach out to schools and other organizations and offer to go to them. A library in Charlotte, North Carolina, offers "Library Resources" as a group visit option. Schools can contact the library and arrange for their group to spend an hour with a library staff member, teaching their students general or specialized research techniques.

Research database navigation, internet privacy, the ability to discern truthful online information: all of these skills are foundational to any post–high school endeavors such as continuing education, vocational training, or entry into the workforce. Teen-serving library staff can play an essential role in ensuring that their community's youth receive this training.

TECHNOLOGY CAREER EXPLORATION WITHIN THE LIBRARY

Libraries can allow teens to explore careers in a safe and friendly environment. A teen who wants to know more about a career in a technological field may not know how best to explore the topic. They may apply for an internship or job without fully understanding the job or its expectations, leading to failure if the young adult ends up unhappy or fired. A much better option is for teen librarians to coordinate teens' opportunities to meet professionals in technological careers or arrange technology-related internships for teens in libraries.

According to the University of California Berkeley Career Center, "Often, the most current information about a career field, especially in a specific geographic location, may not be available online or in books. The best information comes from people who are actually working in that career field."[8] Teens might already have a passion for a potential technology career without a full understanding of what it will take to succeed in that career. There is no better way for them to gain that understanding than to have the opportunity to speak with professionals. As mentioned earlier in the chapter, there is sometimes a gap between the skills required by a new company in a city and the skills possessed by young adults about to enter the workforce. To begin to bridge that gap, invite representatives from local corporations or organizations to come and speak at a program about how they use technology in their jobs and the steps they needed to take to prepare for the role. In this way, teens will do the following:

- Gain an "insider's view" of what it is like to work with technology in various jobs;
- Learn what education or training they will need to succeed in the field;

- Gain an understanding of what employers are looking for in terms of technological skills;
- Form a relationship with someone already working in the career in which they are interested.

Further, the career counselors at the University of California Berkeley also recommend this type of experience as a means of learning more current, relevant information about a topic that may not be published yet. A professional who has recently graduated and begun their career could speak to the recent hiring and education standards employers seek. Someone who has worked in the profession for many years could share what they have done to stay current with continually evolving technology.

Planning for a "Meet a Technology Professional" program (or program series) does not have to be complicated or costly. For inspiration about whom to invite, look no further than the teens who use the library. Ask young library patrons about career goals they have or about careers they want to learn more about if they are not already volunteering that information to teen librarians. Once the librarian knows that their teen patrons are interested in video game development or coding, they can reach out to local organizations to recruit presenters for the program. The program itself does not need to be complicated or expensive. The setup can be chairs in a programming space or the young adult section of the library. The teen librarian can arrange ahead of time with the presenter for any presentation needs they may have and make those available as well. Some teens will choose to attend out of interest in the subject, but some teens may need to be enticed into joining the program with snacks or other small incentives. The presenter may bring small company giveaways to share with the library's patrons.

Once the presenter is set up and the teens have gathered, it is time to begin the program. With the primary objective of introducing teens to a potential career, the professional should spend approximately half the program speaking about their job, education, and day-to-day duties. After that, there will be plenty of time for the participants to ask questions. Some teens could be shy, so the teen librarian can prepare a few questions to get the conversation started.

To fully round out and conclude a "Meet a Technology Professional" program or series of programs, be prepared to collect and forward answers to follow-up questions. If the library system allows, collect email addresses from participants to send them curated suggested further reading lists or links to local training programs or schools that the professional suggests to the group. Even one program that allows teens to meet a technology professional is beneficial; if able, consider offering a series of related programs to multiply the impact. Whole groups of teens get the opportunity to learn more about the technology profession. The teen librarian does the legwork to set it up, and even those teens who may be more reserved or may not have connections with adults in those fields will benefit.

Once a teen has decided that they are interested in a technology career, they may wish to pursue an internship or volunteer opportunity to "try on" the profession. Should they follow this on their own with a company, there is a risk that they could fail and then have wasted time or have a poor reference in their history. However, if the library has a makerspace or offers technology programs, the library can provide teens with opportunities to volunteer or intern with technology programs. When teens volunteer with the library, they do so in a "fail-safe" environment. If they decide the opportunity is not their primary interest, or if they end up unable to fulfill the hours due to school or extracurricular commitments, they can gracefully bow out of the library commitment without nearly as much risk to their budding resumes.

One example of this is an internship that the Loft (a teen-only library space in Charlotte, North Carolina) hosted in 2019. Alexxis L., a master of library and information science student with the University of Alabama, spent a month working alongside Loft staff in their newly established Messy Makerspace. While she was no longer a teen, her experiences in the library could undoubtedly be duplicated for teens, as seen in 2016. In that year, Charlotte Mecklenburg Library secured Dollar General Summer Learning Grant funds to pay two teen interns to work in Idea Box, a makerspace located in the main library branch. In both instances, the interns learned numerous new skills, such as the operation of the vinyl cutters, sewing machines, and design software. Also, they had opportunities to work directly with library patrons and develop their customer-service skills. In Idea Box, the teens worked one-on-one with patrons on their projects; in Messy Makerspace, Alexxis had the opportunity to work with Loft staff to deliver group visits to entire classes of students.

The Loft manager scheduled Alexxis with a more seasoned staff member to bring her up to speed on the software and hardware in the space. This pairing allowed her to ask questions and receive training immediately as she worked with patrons one-on-one or in group settings. Overall, the teen interns and Alexxis gained valuable leadership and teaching skills as they learned in a technology-rich environment. Similarly, many school libraries take on student workers, unpaid, to help with various library tasks, which can include makerspace duties.

Students benefit from these experiences in a variety of ways. They will have the opportunity to learn how to operate the technology and software in the makerspace and provide support to the library staff. As the students begin to build resumes in preparation for paid employment or further educational opportunities, they will list both technological skills and possible leadership skills. Should they be unable to complete the internship for any reason, the only thing that they lose is a potential resume bullet point.

Additionally, librarians are wont to treat every program as a learning opportunity. The teens will receive careful and thorough instruction and shadowing opportunities before they are thrust into leading programs running the makerspace solo. They will be set up for success, not failure, and allowed to explore their technological interests fully.

CONCLUSION

Libraries are ideal places for adolescents to learn vocational readiness skills and to have their first workplace experiences. From their inception, libraries have been seen as a physical space where people of all ages and backgrounds can come to learn the skills necessary to improve their employment opportunities—a real "people's university."[9] Cities across the United States, and in the South, in particular, are discovering that new industries moving in are unable to find local citizens with the appropriate skills to gain employment. Those born at or below the poverty level in these cities are more likely to remain in that socioeconomic group for their whole lives than those who are born into those circumstances elsewhere. Libraries are ideally situated to be classrooms where patrons can be introduced to the skills necessary to move into more technologically advanced careers.

In some cases, libraries are already offering the actual certification courses to their patrons free of charge; others are supplying the resources needed for patrons to pursue independent study. Beyond offering introductions to required technology skills, libraries can also offer young adults the opportunity to "try on" a technology-based job in a failsafe environment. Teen librarians provide instruction in a variety of areas; this can include teaching how to enter the workforce and provide assistance in a technology-rich environment such as a makerspace. Either way, librarians are continuing to serve the purpose of the very earliest public libraries: to provide continuing education resources that allow patrons to prepare for and advance their careers.

NOTES

1. Leading on Opportunity. "Charlotte-Mecklenburg Opportunity Task Force Report." Charlotte-Mecklenburg Opportunity Task Force Report. Accessed June 16, 2020. https://www.leadingonopportunity.org/report/executive-summary.

2. Leading on Opportunity. "Charlotte-Mecklenburg Opportunity Task Force Report."

3. "America Has a Digital Skills Gap. Libraries Can Help Fix It." *The Atlantic*. Accessed June 16, 2020. https://www.theatlantic.com/sponsored/grow-google-2019/america-has-digital-skills-gap-libraries-can-help/3091/.

4. Boston Public Library. *Report of the Trustees of the Public Library to the City of Boston*, 1852. Reproduced in Jesse H. Shera. *Foundations of the Public Library: The Origins of the Public Library Movement in New England, 1629–1855*. University of Chicago Press, 1949; reprint, Chicago: Shoe String Press, 1965, 267–90.

5. "Are There Differences in How Advantaged and Disadvantaged Students Use the Internet?" OECD (Organisation for Economic Co-operation and Development) iLibrary. Accessed June 16, 2020. https://read.oecd-ilibrary.org/education/are-there-differences-in-how-advantaged-and-disadvantaged-students-use-the-internet_5jlv8zq6hw43-en#page4.

6. Herold, Benjamin. "Teens Are Worried about Online Privacy: What Schools Should Do to Protect Them." *Education Week*. May 15, 2018. https://www.edweek.org/technology/teens-are-worried-about-online-privacy-what-schools-should-do-to-protect-them/2018/05.

7. "I AM not the MEdia Workshops." I AM not the MEdia. Accessed June 16, 2020. https://www.iamnotthemedia.org/request-1.

8. University of California Berkeley Career Center. "Informational Interviewing." Accessed August 16, 2019. career.berkeley.edu/info/infointerview.

9. Johnson, Alvin. *The Public Library: A People's University*. New York: American Association for Adult Education, 1938.

SEVEN
Partnerships and Collaboration

It takes a village to raise a child.

—African proverb

When the library partners with the community, both benefit. Collaborating and working together around technology-based purposes can create that needed fuse to spark youth toward further opportunity. We want to be able to leverage these resources to create more on-ramps for youth. In this rapidly changing technology labor market, those that are disconnected need assistance the most. Where do we start?

DEFINING A PARTNERSHIP

I have worked with some organizations—both long- and short-term—where I wondered what the library was getting out of a partnership. I wish I would have recognized some of the signs earlier so that a partnership was more mutually beneficial and perhaps less one-sided. It was a lesson learned to build in some markers along the way to check in with our role and the partner's role to assess what is working and what might need to change if we are to continue.

For example, several years ago when I was the teen librarian for a department at an urban library, I had a professional disc jockey approach me who wanted to do skills-based workshops for the teens for free. He had a curriculum mapped out, was a practicing professional in the field, and would provide the turntables and instructors if we could agree to provide the space for the teens to learn. The arrangement sounded like a great idea. It aligned with the library's focus on connecting teens with their passions and interests. It fit with our schedule on the weekend when we are short-staffed, as it did not require a lot of oversight on our part. Over time, the library's connection with the group was providing free space and a safe place for the youth, but we did not see crossover into other aspects of the library. It was a generous contribution and can be valuable to organizations in the community. But because the teens did not connect with the library outside of this group, I think we could have done more to work together. It began to feel less and less like a real partnership. I think the DJs would have welcomed additional ideas; it was just a matter of evaluating the big picture and then following through by communicating with them.

Like any relationship, a partnership is usually based upon a need, which we will discuss further in this chapter. Regarding technology-based learning and programming, some common bridges to the opportunity gap may look like the following:

- Help reduce or eliminate the digital divide.
- Provide training for those wanting to develop their skills for a career.
- Help teens develop areas of interest through exposure.
- Serve as a conduit for recruiters.
- Offer extended hours for tech resources to be available.
- Develop internship programs for teens wanting experience with assisting the public with technology.

REASONS TO PARTNER

We have just looked at this question from a needs-based standpoint. There are many needs in the community that partnerships can help solve.

At times, it may be tempting to want to do everything on our own. Sometimes developing partnerships might feel like it will take more time than we can or are willing to put forth. But when we see a community problem that can be better solved by working with others, our mindset might shift. The more we start to discover the community's needs, the more we will realize that working with others can enhance what the library can do to effectively reach teens. For example, there is an organization in my community, Eliminate the Digital Divide (E2D https://www.e-2-d.org/[1]), that distributes refurbished computers to those in need at a significantly reduced cost to address the access gap. Twice a year, they partner with the library to give out these laptops to students. Giving the library a role to play in this dispensation helps connect us as a community partner in supporting upward mobility opportunities. Several high schools in the area also have designated computer labs where teens are paid to refurbish the donated computers and learn to make them ready for use. At the same time, E2D has realized that it is putting an affordable computer in the hands of those who might need it and advocating for and making available connectivity access. The quarantine for COVID-19, which started in 2020, has highlighted the fact that families need to know how to use computers. For example, sometimes we assume that people know certain computer skills, such as uploading a file, but that is not necessarily the case. Basic skill training is another opportunity for the library to play a larger role.

If we still have some mixed feelings in developing partnerships and sometimes wanting to do things on our own, we may want to take a moment to reframe what we think a partnership is. There can be several ways that working with others plays out, and they can shift over time as other circumstances change. Whatever baggage we might be bringing with us from a previous partnership that did not work out well, we can learn from our mistakes and continue to move forward. For example, a partnership can be short- or long-term. It can be based on the school year or a summer reading program or even a grant project's duration. It could also have an arbitrary end or break at an agreed-upon time by both partners. You may have a lot on your plate when a potential partner approaches you or vice versa, and perhaps you are unable to work together as much as you would like. That is okay, and things can and should be revised. Be transparent about what you can give in terms of time and resources and guide the collaboration to work for both organizations.

To identify the kind of partnership you are looking for, start with your organization. Your library will likely have criteria of what determines a partnership. For example, when it comes to officially recognizing organizations for their work with the library, you want

Figure 7.1. Working together to make instruments. *Photo by Kelly Czarnecki*

to make sure you are advertising the relationship correctly. Is it a partner, a sponsor, or both, for instance? If you have identified a community need but are not sure how to work with another organization, share questions or concerns you may have with your supervisor or a co-worker for feedback so that you continue to put the best foot forward.

Your library probably has measures in place, such as written agreements or contracts, that are helpful and sometimes needed depending on the library's relationship with the other organization. Learn how your library categorizes partnerships to start. There may be some legacy information about having worked with another organization, and a colleague can share their experience, which may be useful for you. They may also serve as a contact to introduce you to the new person who has taken their place.

DETERMINE COMMUNITY NEED

Chances are that you may be familiar with some community needs, but once you learn more, you discover there are communities of people not known to you.

Starting with what your organization's priorities are can help put you on the right track. If those priorities are not readily apparent, send an email or schedule a meeting with the administration to start a conversation. If the administration is committed to staying relevant to the community, the needs will undoubtedly shift over time. Ask for a time frame: When are priorities reassessed—is it after an annual board meeting, at the start of a new fiscal year, or another time? Your library's priorities may be informed, in part, by local reports. For example, the school system may have a performance report that you can consult online. What are the markers they are holding students accountable to, and are they meeting these goals? If not, how can the library help fill in the gaps?

Sometimes, a national study may have local implications. The Census Report, for example, can be used to better inform the makeup of your community. Also, there was an intergenerational mobility study done in 2013 by researchers at Harvard and UC-Berkeley with findings published the following year: "Where Is the Land of Opportunity? The Geography of Intergenerational Mobility in the United States" (https://scholar.harvard.edu/files/hendren/files/mobility_geo.pdf).[2] Of the fifty largest cities measured, my city placed last. This report resulted in many local leaders coming together to identify strategies to address these findings. The library even created new positions to focus on increasing economic mobility through job help. Technology certainly factored into the plan as well as developing partnerships with companies that held skills-based workshops. Ask questions of leadership about what drives priorities and freely share community reports with co-workers, if they are not already informed, as they become relevant.

NOTES

1. E2D. Accessed September 28, 2020. https://www.e-2-d.org/.
2. Raj Chetty et al. (June 2014). "Where Is the Land of Opportunity? The Geography of Intergenerational Mobility in the United States." Harvard and University of California Berkeley. https://scholar.harvard.edu/files/hendren/files/mobility_geo.pdf.

Part III

Technology in Practice

EIGHT
Tech without Tech

Have you ever considered how you might be able to offer technology-centric programs in your library without the ability or permission to utilize actual technology? You may facilitate programs in your library or community that would fall under the subject heading of "technology" or have a primary learning objective of "technology," but do not use devices requiring plugs, chargers, or internet access. Technology programs that involve few materials and no plugs are easily transportable if you are doing outreach. These programs are also very low cost, if not free, and there are more options than you may be aware of. They are excellent choices for those who are just starting their technology or makerspace endeavors or facilitating several programs out in their community.

Low cost will, of course, be a primary reason to consider offering techless technology programs to your patrons. The program ideas that follow will not hit your budget hard. Common materials required for these programs include paper, writing implements, batteries, copper tape, or materials from your recycling bin. In the following sections, you will read ideas for activities that call for no materials at all. Perhaps you are just beginning to set up your library's makerspace or start a series of technology-focused programs. You will want to be cautious with your budget, and these activities will allow you to expand your offerings greatly without additional expense.

A further reason for offering low- or no-tech technology programs would be due to storage space. Not every library has a fully established, permanent makerspace or technology center. Even those who do have these spaces may not be able to staff them fully and need activities to offer that require little or no staff assistance. Suppose you are working with a community room or other library space shared with children's or adult programs and must store your program supplies between uses. In that case, you will want to minimize the number of physical materials needed. The rest of the chapter's activities offer you various options that utilize the same set of space-saving, low-cost materials. Furthermore, they require little or no setup. There is no making sure that devices are charged ahead of time and no elaborate preparation of the materials. You can have programs ready to go out of a bin in your office. Any time there are groups of teens in your library, you will be able to pull out a ready-to-go activity to engage them.

One final but very important reason for having mobile, low-tech programs is outreach, especially to vulnerable populations. In their book *Serving At-Risk Teens: Proven Strategies and Programs for Bridging the Gap*, Angela Craig and Chantell L. McDowell dedicate a chapter to the critical impact library staff can have when they travel to youth facilities and provide outreach. There are many types of youth facilities: alternative schools, counseling centers, emergency shelters, group homes, and juvenile detention centers. Many of these facilities will require that visiting library staff adhere to their schedules and parameters. You may not be permitted to bring in computers, tablets, or other devices that could connect to the internet. You may not be allowed to bring any materials into some places, such as in-patient counseling centers or juvenile detention centers. You may be required to let them know of needs, such as paper or writing implements, so that the facility can provide them. Even if you visit a facility that allows you to bring in your own materials, you will likely not want to transport large pieces of equipment and may still not be allowed to bring in internet-connecting devices.[1]

In the remainder of the chapter, you will gain insights into why you might choose to offer low- or no-tech technology programs to teen patrons both in your library space and in other community spaces where teens gather. You will save funds, space, and preparation time and become flexible in when and where you offer your programs.

TECHNOLOGY AS A MEANS OF FACILITATING CRITICAL THINKING AND DISCUSSION

Technology is ever-present in teens' lives. It is as familiar to them as their socks. Because of this, technology and technological advances can be an excellent foundation for discussions about broader issues and encourage critical thinking and debate. Take, for instance, the advances in facial recognition software in the late 2010s. This technology allowed for extra security in phone locks, and users waved at their smart screens to turn programs on and off. Teens (just like many adults) were quite excited about it and could not wait to get the latest iPhone. As a teen program facilitator, you can ask teens to think critically about this software. Can they name any potential negatives to the software? In early 2019, San Francisco became the first American city to ban the software's use by police or other government agencies.[2] Will the teens be able to tell you why that might be? While it is an older book, *Little Brother* by Cory Doctorow would be an excellent pairing for this topic.

In our work, we saw a program offered periodically called "Guy Talk." This program was often informal and unplanned and would occur when several young people were hanging out in our teen space, open to discussion and light mentorship. One of our colleagues, Jay Pendergrass, would join them, offering snacks and conversation. This type of questioning is a perfect fit for a conversational discussion program. While the teens are relaxing and engaging with an adult role model, they are also learning critical thinking and debate skills. Think of college admissions, SAT/ACT exams, and AP classes: Teens will be asked to think critically and write short essays expressing opinions. These conversations over chips and soda could positively impact their future.

Another way to introduce critical thinking about technology-related current issues is through a book club discussion of *Little Brother* by Cory Doctorow, *Unwind* by Neal Shusterman, or *Uglies* by Scott Westerfeld. All these titles deal with the theme of misuse of technology by government agencies. You do not need to have a regularly occurring book club to host a book discussion. A single-event book discussion can break the routine of other programs, draw a crowd, and provoke great conversation. A book discussion outside of a regularly occurring book club can highlight the event and attract new participants. Remain aware of new titles with a theme of government misuse of technological power and use these to fuel the discussion.

This program is ideal for outreach to facilities where teens may not have full access to actual technological devices, such as incarcerated youth or youth undergoing mental health treatments. Of course, these teens are still very interested in and aware of technological advances and are often eager to discuss them. Either the informal conversation or the book-based discussion works well in these types of outreach scenarios. Again, teens are gaining critical thinking skills while enjoying time spent with a teen-serving library staff member.

Whether your teens are in your library or out in the community, conversations around technological advances are a way to deepen your relationships and teach critical thinking skills. We recommend structuring the conversations around current events, new consumer technology available on the market, or books that touch on similar themes. You do not need any specialized training or materials to facilitate these discussions, and they do not necessarily even need to be planned and marketed in advance. While teens gain the skills necessary to think and write critically, you will deepen relationships with your teen population.

"To every action there is an equal and opposite reaction."[3] Similarly, there will always be detractors to any new development or invention. Often this is beneficial, as those who question new ideas can help the developers fine-tune new inventions. In the following case, the detractors question the social and mental health benefits of technology in teens' lives. The *American Journal of Epistemology* conducted an international study that linked increased social media use with increased mental health problems in youth.[4] They found that the pressures of "performance" online—always to project a happy, successful life—created high stress levels. Furthermore, technology use has been linked to shortened attention spans and multitasking attempts, leading to errors in work.[5]

This information, replicated in other studies, has many adults who work with teens thinking about how teens use technology and how to influence safe and productive use. We teen-serving library staff can help our young customers become civil digital citizens and responsible digital leaders, which can have a genuine and vital impact on our society. In 2018, 59 percent of American teenagers reported to a Pew Research study that they had been cyberbullied in one way or another.[6] There are many positives to the current technology access levels, such as communicating quickly and strengthening in-person relationships or gaining access to round-the-clock educational support. Still, there is also an opportunity for those who work with teens to influence their behaviors and shape them into mindful, respectful digital citizens.

"There is an important difference between 'online safety' and 'digital citizenship,'" Richard Culatta, CEO of the International Society for Technology in Education, states. He goes on to elaborate that much of current online safety guidelines are lists of "don'ts," such as "don't share passwords," "don't share personal information," "don't be a cyberbully," etc. Instead, he proposes that educators and caregivers teach students positive actions that they can take when utilizing technology. If done correctly and thoroughly, the impact will extend past their participation in online communities and lead to four outcomes:

> Improvement in students' real-world communities, improvement in students' ability to shape public policy, more respectful online engagement with those who hold different beliefs, and improved ability to determine the validity of information online. . . . Digital citizenship is not about teaching curriculum—it's about creating a culture. . . . We have to make good digital citizens . . . that know how to enrich community through technology—not just exist in it.[7]

As a teen-serving library staff member, there is an opportunity to have these conversations with students and shape their thinking about their digital citizenship. The conversations can focus on the positives. Challenge your teen patrons to think of what it would look like to be a good friend online. Instead of continually saying that they should not be a cyberbully, help them see what actions they can take today to demonstrate civility in their online interactions. Another frequent admonition to teens is this: Do not give out personal information online. Think of how that can be rephrased into a positive action. You might remind teens that they are unique and have a personal "brand" to protect. Just as they would not design the next big footwear and then give out the design and pattern for free online, they should not divulge everything that identifies and makes up themselves on the internet.

Discussions around appropriate new technology use can be just as engaging as programs involving actual physical pieces of technology and hold educational value. Participating teens will learn to think critically about the world around them and their roles in digital interactions. Further, they will have the opportunity to develop relationships with peers and potential mentors among the group and with the library leader. These programs, which can take place in your library or the community, are inexpensive and rewarding.

TECHNOLOGY-BASED OUTREACH PROGRAMMING

Some teens are unable to come to your physical library location. In those cases, you will need to go to the teens. There are numerous reasons why a youth cannot get to a library. It may be that they do not have reliable access to transportation. Even if they can drive, they may not have their own vehicle. It could be that they are receiving services from other teen-serving organizations while your library is open. Many organizations are clamoring for teens' attention in the hours after school: sports teams, tutoring centers, religious groups, scouts, and other hobbies. Or it might be that they are currently residing in a group home, alternative school, or juvenile detention center and do not have the option to travel to a library, even with their group. Whatever the reason, you may find yourself going to your teen population rather than welcoming them to your library space.

There are a few things that you will want to consider when planning your outreach programs. No matter the group, you will need to choose efficient, scalable, and complete activities. Efficient: your program should contain as few pieces as possible. The less material required, the less likely you are to forget something back at the office. Fewer items need to be prepared and packed, reducing your preparation time. You are already spending time traveling to the location; there is no need to spend much time preparing. As you hold outreach programs, take note of the most successful ones. It is worth considering creating a ready-to-go box with supplies for those programs so that you can accept outreach requests more often or support your colleagues. The box might contain instructions, lesson objectives, and needed supplies. You or a colleague can pull it out any time you have an unexpected group of teens in your library space or when you are asked to do outreach at another facility.

Just as no two library branches are identical, no two teen-serving organizations are identical. A good outreach program will be scalable to match the competencies of the students you are meeting and the size of their group. Squishy Circuits, explained more fully later in the chapter, are a good example of scalability. To create the squishy dough, you will need to have a ratio of ingredients. The facilitator can make a small batch using the base ratio or multiply to create a larger quantity. The activities that the students then complete using the electricity-conducting dough can also be scaled to ability. Younger students may create a circuit that lights up a small light bulb. Older students can be given more complex challenges to complete.

Since the program is being done off-site and the youth are not guaranteed quick access to you again, you will want to make sure that the participants can fully complete the activity in the time allotted. The other location staff may not feel confident walking the students through finishing steps, and the organization may not have storage space for items. The youth present may not be consistent visit to visit either. Ensuring that the activity is simple enough to be completed in one session will ensure higher satisfaction levels than half-completed projects.

Before planning an outreach activity for a group, speak to the other organization's program leaders. They will be able to tell you of any restrictions. You can also describe the activity to them to ask for feedback on their youth's skill level. Once you know the group's expected size, ages, and skill level, you will be better equipped to choose an activity that meets their needs. Some organizations may tell you that their youth are not allowed to have even low-tech technology. Other organizations may ask for a list of supplies and then provide those for you. At the other end of the spectrum, there will be groups who have little or no restrictions. This initial conversation also allows for expectations to be set; for example, it might be requested that a certain number of staff from the other organization remain present in the room or even hands-on with assisting.

Some of the best technology outreach activities will involve low-tech devices or no technology at all. There are fewer potential fail points this way. There is nothing worse than arriving at an outreach location with devices that require the internet and finding that the location has no Wi-Fi. Further advantages are that these program ideas are likely to be acceptable even in more controlled environments and enjoyable by any group. Any program idea described later in this chapter would fit these criteria.

TECHLESS AND LOW-TECH ACTIVITIES FOR MAKERSPACES

Libraries everywhere are adding makerspaces, both formal and informal. These will be discussed in much more detail in the following chapter, but it is worth noting that many makerspaces offer much more than 3D printers. Library staff nationwide are offering low-tech or no-tech programs and activities in these spaces as well, creating a threshold low enough for even the newest makers to feel comfortable. When new to makerspaces, some visitors could feel overwhelmed with the larger technology, such as 3D printers and laser cutters. Seeing opportunities for themselves with more familiar analog tools such as paper, paint, and scissors will create a more welcoming environment.

During the research for this book, the authors used a survey to gather information from teen-serving library staff members across America. Among survey respondents, approximately 50 percent had makerspaces in their libraries. These makerspaces ranged from carts that were brought out intermittently to dedicated rooms. Many of these same respondents mentioned simple crafts as part of their regular offerings connected to the makerspace. Some of these libraries also offered technology-related programs that did not use complicated devices.

Simple, analog crafts that might be offered in makerspaces include supplies for knitting or crocheting; paper, craft knives, markers, paints, and scissors for paper crafts; and beads, wire, and filament for jewelry making. These are implements that visitors would readily recognize and quite possibly already know how to use. Not every makerspace will have dedicated staff, and having out simple supplies will allow the space to be used even during those times when trained personnel are not present to operate the larger machines. When the library provides the low-tech materials and instructions for simple projects, they become more inviting to all. There are many other advantages to stocking your mobile or permanent makerspace with analog craft supplies: for example, the same tools are used for a large variety of projects, and these supplies are mobile. Should a library have a low budget for maker activities, a selection of analog supplies provides the basis for hundreds of projects. Think of all that can be created from colored paper and adhesive or with yarn and crochet hooks.

Traditional crafts can serve as entry points into the maker culture for many. Consider how many simple crafts can be scaled upward into technology instruction. Let us use paper greeting cards as an example. Most library users would feel immediately comfortable using paper, pens, scissors, and the like to create traditional greeting cards. To use this craft as a foundation for teaching technology skills, a librarian might introduce copper tape, LED lights, and coin cell batteries to the available pool of supplies. With these additions, participants could be taught to create simple circuits and make cards that light up. Alternatively, library staff could use the desire to create greeting cards to teach design on computers and assist patrons with creating printable cards with custom designs or making designs executable on a Cricut or similar machine. The magazine *Make:* recommends having traditional, low-tech materials on hand in your makerspace as a means of inclusivity.[8] The author of the article, Becky LeBret, gives an example of mobile makerspace carts even being instituted in children's hospitals when they include lower-tech options. Suppose you want your makerspace to be portable, able to function or be accessible with little or no staff oversight, and inexpensive to start. In that case, low-tech traditional crafting supplies are a solid foundation.

These low-tech crafts also lend themselves readily to storage on a mobile cart, in bins or drawers in a permanent maker area, or in supply closets in permanent makerspaces. Because so many of these craft supplies have multiple uses, you do not need a large amount. A librarian could stock the lowest cost, most efficient items in various colors and not give up much storage space. In the final section of this chapter, there will be several low-tech ideas that a maker-oriented librarian can implement with simple, cheap tradi-

Figure 8.1.   Example of paper circuits. *Photo by Marie Harris*

tional craft supplies. The greatest advantages of purchasing these materials are the low cost and the invitation to even the newest potential makers.

TECHNOLOGY PROGRAMS WITHOUT TECHNOLOGY

This section explores tried-and-tested ideas for technology and maker programs that involve little or no devices. As discussed earlier, there are many reasons to utilize these ideas. A teen-serving librarian may need to have activities ready for outreach visits to locations that do not have technology or allow technology use by their wards. They may be starting maker carts or makerspaces with a limited budget. Or they may want to expand their current offerings. No matter your reasoning, these activities will help to get you started.

- **Dry Ice Bubble Generator.** Teaches: reactions, cause and effect, pathways. Supplies: empty disinfectant wipe containers, lengths of rubber tubing, dry ice, warm water, dish soap. Cut a small opening on the container's side near the top and insert a rubber tubing piece. Put a small piece of dry ice in the container. Dip the loose end of the rubber tubing in dish soap and pour warm water into the container. The mist from the dry ice melting will travel through the tube and meet the dish-soap-coated end of the tube and bubbles will form, filled with dry ice mist[9] (see project on p. 82).
- **Origami.** Teaches: angles, geometry. Supplies: paper of various weights and colors. Many books and online instructions are available to teach a multitude of folding patterns. The participant begins with a sheet of paper and produces a three-dimensional object through a series of folds.
- **Paper Circuits.** Teaches: electric circuitry. Supplies: paper of various weights and colors, copper tape, coin cell batteries, LED lights with exposed circuitry. This project can be used at any time of the year for any reason. It also works well during holidays in the creation of greeting cards. Participants learn that they can create a circuit using copper tape that is adhered to paper. When the copper tape touches both sides of a coin cell battery and both exposed legs of an LED light, the light will glow. Participants can create greeting cards with lit features on the front, as the copper tape will create a circuit when the card is closed, and both sides of the paper are touching. Simple folds in a sheet of paper will produce the same circuit, without the greeting card aspect.[10]
- **Squishy Circuits.** Teaches: electric circuitry. Supplies: flour, salt, water, cream of tartar, sugar, vegetable oil, wires with alligator clip ends, coin cell batteries, LED lights with exposed circuitry. First, you make the conductive dough by combining 1½ cups flour, ¼ cup salt, 1 tablespoon cream of tartar, 1 cup water, and 2 tablespoons vegetable oil. Next, you will make the insulating dough by combining 1½ cups flour, ½ cup sugar, 3 tablespoons vegetable oil, and ½ cup water. Finally, you lead participants in creating electrical circuits utilizing the pliable dough, wires, lights, and batteries. There are many resources and project ideas available on the internet[11] (see project on p. 87).

CONCLUSION

Librarians do not need to have a large budget, an abundance of storage space, or even an electrical outlet to provide technology-focused programs to their teenaged customers inside their branch and in their communities. The goal is to introduce teens to technology in whatever manner best fits your community and library. Some libraries may be small, without a dedicated makerspace or technology lab. This chapter's ideas use materials that can be rearranged to suit several different projects and do not require much space to store. Some librarians may work in their communities rather than in a brick-and-mortar library. Rather than relying on other organizations' technology, electricity, and the internet, these program ideas will allow the librarian to focus on technology without charging any devices or worrying about weak Wi-Fi signals. For these reasons and many more, teen-serving library staff can use tech-without-tech program ideas to kick-start discussions and learning with their patrons.

NOTES

1. Craig, Angela, and Chantell L. McDowell. *Serving At-Risk Teens: Proven Strategies and Programs for Bridging the Gap*. Chicago: American Library Association, 2013. Accessed October 9, 2019. ProQuest Ebook Central.
2. Conger, Kate, Richard Fausset, and Serge F. Kovaleski. "San Francisco Bans Facial Recognition Technology." *The New York Times*. May 14, 2019. https://www.nytimes.com/2019/05/14/us/facial-recognition-ban-san-francisco.html.
3. "Newton's Laws of Motion." *Oxford Reference*. Accessed October 9, 2019. https://www.oxfordreference.com/view/10.1093/oi/authority.20110803100232420.
4. "New Studies Show That Social Media Has Become a Global Mental Health Problem for Younger Generations." *PR Newswire*. March 29, 2018. http://nclive.org/cgi-bin/nclsm?url=http://search.proquest.com/docview/2019248929?accountid=13217.
5. Harrold, Mark. "How to Tame Teenagers' Technology Use in the Digital Age." *Irish Times*. November 8, 2016. http://nclive.org/cgi-bin/nclsm?url=http://search.proquest.com/docview/1836817773?accountid=13217.
6. Anderson, Monica. "A Majority of Teens Have Experienced Some Form of Cyberbullying." Pew Research Center: Internet & Technology. September 27, 2018. https://www.pewinternet.org/2018/09/27/a-majority-of-teens-have-experienced-some-form-of-cyberbullying/.
7. Johnston, Ryan. "Digital Citizenship Is More Than Staying Safe Online, Says ISTE's Chief Executive." *EdScoop*. March 4, 2019. https://edscoop.com/digital-citizenship-is-more-than-staying-safe-online-urges-istes-chief-executive/.
8. LeBret, Becky. "Want to Create a Budget-Friendly Makerspace in the New Year? Think, Plan, and Organize." *Make:*. January 12, 2018. https://makezine.com/2018/01/12/want-create-budget-friendly-makerspace-new-year-think-plan-organize/.
9. "Bouncing Smoke Bubbles (Boo Bubbles)." Steve Spangler Science: The Lab. Accessed June 17, 2020. https://www.stevespanglerscience.com/lab/experiments/boo-bubbles-dry-ice-science/.
10. "Paper Circuits for Makerspaces." Makerspaces.com. February 7, 2018. Accessed June 18, 2020. https://www.makerspaces.com/paper-circuits/.
11. "Invent. Create. Explore." Squishy Circuits. Accessed June 18, 2020. https://squishycircuits.com/.

NINE

Making, Makerspaces, and the Maker Movement

Sharona Ginsberg, a learning technologies librarian at State University of New York (SUNY) at Oswego, defines a *makerspace* as follows:

> Any area where people gather to make and create. These spaces often include 3D printers but do not necessarily have to. In makerspaces, people share supplies, skills, and ideas and often work together on projects. Makerspaces grew out of maker culture—a group of people dedicated to craftsmanship and creation. Makerism focuses on DIY projects, and makers value creation by individuals or small groups rather than bulk production. In general, makerism is also a culture of creation over consumption.[1]

As you can see from this definition, a makerspace does not need to be a set, physical space. A makerspace can be any space, at any time, in which people gather to share supplies and create new things. Some libraries will be fortunate to have a dedicated space in which maker materials and equipment are available at all or nearly all times. These spaces can contain larger pieces of technology, such as 3D printers, laser cutters, or CNC routers, and accompanying computers to complete the design work with which to operate them. Librarians can facilitate maker activities with technology, even without a dedicated space.

The Maker Movement began in the early 2000s. It is difficult to pinpoint an exact date on which people across America began to recognize the terms "maker," "makerspace," and "Maker Faire." We know that MIT's Fab Lab opened in 2001 and was one of the first popularly talked about makerspaces. We know that *Make:* magazine launched in 2005, and the first Maker Faire was held in San Mateo, California, in 2006.[2] From this, it would be safe to say that making most likely began in grassroots movements across the country in the late 1990s and solidified into a movement in the early 2000s.

Making inspires creativity and more. The movement encourages its participants to be active creators as opposed to passive consumers. One early article predicted that the maker movement would lead to micromanufacturing and the end of mass productions.[3] While we have not seen major manufacturers' demise, we have seen the rise of small business creation, prototyping, and personalized production. Examples include microbusiness aggregates such as Etsy.com, where home-based creative business owners offer unique solutions and personalized items.

Makerspaces, and the nurturing of the maker culture, go hand in hand with library missions. Libraries exist to promote literacy and inspire learning and creativity. The maker movement shares these goals as it encourages the growth of creative literacy. While some makerspace users will create seemingly simple projects or re-create 3D prints that others have designed, other users will produce functional items that improve their own or others' lives.[4] Librarians who encourage the creation of makerspaces and maker culture in their library spaces foster creativity and innovation.

ESTABLISHING A LIBRARY MAKERSPACE

Starting a makerspace can bring both excitement and trepidation. Librarians are correct to get excited about sharing maker resources with their patrons. The activities offered in these environments promote creativity, teach problem-solving skills, and can be foundational for educational success. Even beyond that, the programs are fun.

Before jumping into cultivating ideas for maker programs, the library needs to determine how their makerspace will look. There is no one correct way to make in libraries. The makerspace might be a large, dedicated space full of technology, tools, and well-trained staff. It may be a small utility cart filled with analog tools and craft supplies facilitated by programming library staff. The space can be anything in between as well. Consider the space available in the library and any upcoming renovations. Some library staff may be limited to start maker activities in a small area with no plans to expand. Other library staff are on the verge of renovation periods and may advocate for the creation of a dedicated makerspace area.

As the space decision is made, strongly consider surveying your existing patrons and makers in your community to determine what type of space will best serve your area. When Richland County, South Carolina, began planning the renovation of their main library, they knew that they wanted to include a makerspace. As architectural plans were drawn up, staff surveyed their existing customers to determine what aspects of the maker movement appealed to them. Next, they surveyed members of the community who were not necessarily regular library users at the time but who had the potential to become stakeholders in the makerspace, such as local craftspeople and small business owners. These potential stakeholders were asked the same questions. This information was then used to create a makerspace that has seen a large amount of use and impact on the community. For example, the staff learned that there was no great interest in 3D printers, but there was a lot of interest in woodworking. With this information, they were able to allocate equipment purchases to allow for more woodworking tools. When working with teens, it is recommended that regular teen patrons are surveyed. The additional stakeholders that might be surveyed are school libraries that have maker activities or other youth-serving organizations interested in becoming users of the makerspace. This step is critical and will ensure that library staff create a space used by the community.

Creating a makerspace (or maker cart) will be an exercise in problem-solving. Once you have considered your library's physical space parameters and have collected data from current and potential stakeholders, you will need to consider your budget. Have you been granted a lump sum start-up budget? Will the budget be renewed each year for the replenishment of supplies? Is a staff member (or more than one) allocated within the budget? It is important to know the answers to these questions before planning. The answers will determine what equipment you might purchase, depending on whether you will secure additional supplies as they are used. It may also prove too intimidating to purchase equipment such as a laser cutter or 3D printer if you cannot afford staff time for adequate training and oversight.

Speaking of staff oversight, librarians need to take into consideration staff in the makerspace. Few libraries seem to be fortunate enough to be granted the funding for staff dedicated to a makerspace. Staff may need to be shared with other departments and branch functions. The following section describes a selection of makerspaces in Charlotte Mecklenburg Library branches, few of which have staff assigned entirely to the spaces. Some alternatives to paid staff for all branch open hours would be to utilize volunteers or to have the makerspace portion of the library open for fewer hours than the rest of the library branch.

CASE STUDY: MAKERSPACES IN CHARLOTTE MECKLENBURG LIBRARY BRANCHES

At the time of this writing, the Charlotte Mecklenburg Library system in Charlotte, North Carolina, has twenty branches, and four of them contain makerspaces. As we are writing this book, at least one more branch is under renovation and receiving a makerspace. Each of the existing makerspaces is unique. Each makerspace meets the needs of each community rather than duplicating the same model across the county.

ImaginOn, the exclusively youth-serving branch located in Charlotte's center, is home to both the very first and one of the latest established makerspaces. The branch opened in October 2005 with a digital media creation space in their teen area called Studio i. Walking upstairs to the Teen Loft, library patrons ages ten to eighteen[5] can cross the space into a large room filled with all the equipment teens need to create movies, music, and more. The space includes an entire wall painted blue to act as a blue screen, a ReadyANIMATOR for stop-motion animation films, computers for editing footage, a recording booth with a microphone for recording vocals or instrumentals, and an electric keyboard. Teen patrons can also find staff and teenage volunteers ready to assist and teach, pre-recorded beat loops that can have vocals added, and an assortment of costumes. While all this equipment is available regularly to walk-in patrons, the Teen Loft staff also offer group visits to the local school and community organization groups. All staff who work in the Loft department take shifts working in Studio i, which is open on weekday and Saturday afternoons only.

Idea Box was the next Charlotte Mecklenburg Library makerspace. This makerspace opened in January 2015 and is located within the main library branch, just a block away from ImaginOn. While Studio i limits the ages of users to teenagers, Idea Box welcomes teens and adults. This makerspace was designed to resemble many other library makerspaces at the time. It contains counter-height tables for drafting, planning, and assembly; a small bank of computers with design software; three 3D printers; a laser cutter; a vinyl cutter; and a host of woodworking and craft tools. Charlotte Mecklenburg Library emphasizes programs in the makerspace that teach transferable skills for future careers and promotes the use of the computerized or digital equipment in the space. This makerspace is the one that has a dedicated staff member who is available during Idea Box operating hours to assist patrons through the use of all the equipment. Idea Box cannot be open all the hours that the main library is open with a single staff member; instead, it is open on select afternoons and evenings each week.

SouthPark Regional Library, a branch located in the south part of the county, was the next library to gain a makerspace in 2018. Like Idea Box, SouthPark's makerspace is open to both teenagers and adults. Several staff at SouthPark self-selected to receive training on the equipment's operation in the space and rotate assisting patrons interested in visiting the space. This makerspace is one of the smallest among the Charlotte Mecklenburg libraries in a single classroom-sized room. It boasts a 3D printer, Carvey, vinyl cutter, and sewing machine. Interested patrons request access to the makerspace at the reference desk

Figure 9.1. High school students in multimedia makerspace Studio i. *Photo by Marie Harris*

and are granted entrance if any trained staff are available to assist. If no one is available, appointments can be made to return, but this rarely happens.

Also in 2018, ImaginOn gained a second makerspace. The equipment is referred to as Messy Makerspace. This one is unique in that all the equipment is on wheels. While there is a dedicated classroom-sized room in which to store the equipment, all working surfaces and equipment can be easily rolled into the open public space. The classroom is available if needed to limit the class size or contain noise; otherwise, creation occurs in public areas. Counter-height workstations, iPads for design work, two 3D printers, and a vinyl cutter can all travel.

Additionally, this makerspace boasts a screenprinting apparatus for adding custom logos or artwork to fabrics. Like Studio i, all Loft staff are expected to take turns staffing Messy Makerspace when it is open. Messy Makerspace is open many Saturdays to the general public and select times during the week for programs or group visits by schools or community organizations. Also like Studio i and the rest of the Loft, Messy Makerspace is age-limited to patrons ages ten to eighteen. With this space dedicated entirely to teen use, every effort is made to draw young adults' attention. There is a display case just outside the room showcasing things made in Messy Makerspace that will appeal to teens. All the walls inside are painted vibrant colors and covered with relevant contemporary images and quotes.

The North County Regional Library, located in Huntersville, North Carolina, was the latest branch to gain a makerspace in 2019. This makerspace consists of many connected parts: a work or design area with counter-height tables and stools continually open to all library users; a classroom-sized room with microphones, computers, and editing software for podcast creation; and a classroom-sized room with two 3D printers, a Carvey, and a vinyl cutter. The two equipment rooms are locked except when a staff member is present. Just as at SouthPark, staff self-selected for training to work in the space and assist patrons. Additionally, the branch manager sought to hire staff members in youth and adult services who had an openness to making.

A further similarity to SouthPark is in open hours: there are no regularly occurring open, walk-in hours. Patrons interested in utilizing the makerspace or equipment will need to make an appointment, handled via an online scheduling tool. This tool asks the patron to choose which pieces of equipment they will be using. The library branch customizes which time slots are available when the patrons choose each piece of equipment, guaranteeing that a staff member familiar with the equipment will be working at that time. Even though the branch asks that patrons make appointments for more intensive assistance, the counter-height collaboration tables are always available. All staff can give interested patrons a quick tour of the available equipment.

These unique makerspaces contain various equipment, so patrons of all ages will find a space that meets their needs. All of these spaces have staff who are passionate about making and knowledgeable about the equipment. The spaces also have group library programs to introduce patrons of all ages to the spaces and equipment, and there are no makerspace charges for materials consumed while in library programs.[6] The variety in layout and open hours means that teens can find the materials or guidance they need at a time that fits their schedules.

MAKER PROGRAM PARAMETERS

Often when those who are unfamiliar with makerspaces think of maker activities, they envision a space filled with raw materials and unknown equipment. There may or may not be example projects in the space or projects-in-process awaiting their creator's return. For the uninitiated, the first visit or two can be intimidating. The patron may feel pressure to decide upon a project without being fully aware of the potential of the materials and equipment. One way to help invite teens into a makerspace is to offer programs that teach a specific skill while tackling a clearly defined problem. For example, you can introduce teens to Makey Makey or Arduino technology by inviting them to create audible components for tactile picture books, which are picture books for children living with visual challenges. In this example, you are teaching the use of a new piece of equipment (Makey Makeys or Arduinos) to teens with a purpose (narration of picture books so that those who cannot see well can still enjoy the book). At the end of the session, you can ask teens to reflect on how else they may use this new skill or new technology. Can they imagine creating cosplay pieces with auditory components for an upcoming convention?

While you and your teen patrons are having fun creating in the makerspace, remember that you are also fulfilling your library's mission and making an impression upon the patrons' educational success and workforce development skills. Library mission statements and how they relate to technology use in libraries are discussed in more depth in chapter 4. In general, the conclusion is that many library missions speak to the goals of improving lives or furthering education. Makerspaces support the mission of libraries by teaching problem-solving skills or digital literacy readiness. These skills are then transferrable to educational success or first jobs. Think also of the entrepreneurship opportunities when teens learn how to create custom projects in a makerspace. Among the many projects on display outside of Messy Makerspace at ImaginOn are T-shirts and binders with individualized iron-on or sticker designs. An intrepid teen could create and then resell their unique creations.

Keep continuity in mind as makerspace programs are designed and facilitated. When Idea Box at the Main Library first opened, the team of staff who worked in the space created detailed lesson plans for each program and shared them to Google Drive. In this way, an extensive library of programs was built over time.

The lesson plans gave a title, a program description that could be copied and pasted into the library's event calendar, a recommended maximum number of participants, a per-participant cost, a list of needed materials and equipment, instructions, and slides (if needed). When one staff member had a successful program, another staff member could replicate the program later using the instructions. One example of this was the perennially popular "3D Printing 101." In this program, participants learn how the space's 3D printers work and could get started on designing and printing their first projects. See this lesson plan as an example:

Title: 3D Printing 101

Program Description: An introduction to 3D printing in Idea Box. No experience necessary.

Number of Attendees: Six

Price per Participant: < $5 (dependent upon the size of an object designed for printing)

Supplies: (6) hot glue guns; (6 or more) hot glue gun sticks; (6) flexible cutting mats; PC for every 1–2 participants; filament for 3D printing; (1) 3D printer

Supplemental Materials: 3D Printing 101 Handout

Program Outline:

- *Before program:* Plug in hot glue guns to begin heating
- Welcome and introduction
- Hot glue guns to illustrate the concept of 3D printing
    - Instruct participants to draw multiple straight lines on their mat: a fat one, a thin one, and one that is as uniform as possible. Discuss what makes the lines different shapes and what technique produces the most uniform line. Relate this to how the extruder on the MakerBot lays down the filament in a 3D print.
    - Instruct participants to draw an uppercase "I" that is hollow and then fill it in. Talk to the participants about different techniques they used and relate it to how the MakerBot initializes print jobs.
- 3D printer introduction
    - Introduce participants to the 3D printers. Show them the various parts and their names, such as the nozzle, the extruder (and tell them never to remove the extruder), the knob, the USB port.
    - Demonstrate how to remove and insert the filament into the extruder safely. (Tell participants never to do this without Idea Box staff.)
    - Begin a sample print.
- Designing
    - Introduce participants to MakerBot Desktop.
    - Introduce participants to Thingiverse.
    - Introduce participants to TinkerCad and Autodesk.
- *End of program:* All participants can submit their designs for printing (and later pickup) or be given coupons for a free < $5 print later.

Whether participants were just getting started or wanted to get their first print at the library for free, registration filled up every time this class was offered. One staff member alone may not have been able to meet the demand. Furthermore, at the start, Idea Box was staffed entirely by staff from other departments or even other branches who volunteered a few hours a week in the space. The team membership rotated occasionally. As new members joined the team, they could access the library of programs and jump right into productively contributing to the calendar of events. Your space may be the same; it may be staffed by one or more members who have primary roles outside of the makerspace, or it may be assisted in staffing by volunteers. With a library of successfully tried-and-tested programs, any person who staffs the space can replicate a program, and service continuity to your patrons is provided.

The creation of lesson plans within set parameters that meet your library's mission will ensure the continuity of excellent service to your teen customers. They allow new staff in the space or volunteers to deliver popular or recurring programs from the start of their service. The lesson plans also serve as a checkpoint to ensure the makerspace programs remain aligned to your library's mission.

INCLUSIVITY

A further consideration as a library plans for a makerspace is inclusivity, especially important for teen patrons. During adolescence, teens discover their identities (in many aspects) and experience peer pressure or even outright bullying in many other areas. Librarians are trusted adults in teens' lives, and libraries are often seen as a safe space for teens who do not fit elsewhere.

An independent makerspace was founded in North Carolina in the early 2010s as a nonprofit that invited open access to membership to persons of all ages. The founding members were dissatisfied with other local makerspace options that offered membership only to adults. They saw the potential in providing services and opportunities to youth, as do many public libraries, and so began their makerspace. It was not long before the question of vulnerable individuals arose. Thanks to their completely open membership invitation, several families with teenage children living with autism began utilizing the space. Eventually, teenagers with autism began enjoying the space as a group or individually with inadequate adult supervision. The entirely volunteer staff in the space felt overwhelmed, as these members frequently needed more assistance than others. The decision was made by the board of directors to individually contact the families of the higher-need members and encourage them to either provide assistance or drop their membership. At least one member of the board of directors chose to distance themselves from the organization following this decision, stating that they would have preferred to offer assistance to higher-need members through other means such as the "hiring" of more volunteers during high-use times.

This story illustrates the increasingly common awareness of the need to provide support to those customers who may have special or extended needs. Makerspaces can provide creative outlets for those who may not have "voices" in more traditional spaces. Libraries should keep in mind potential users who would need assistance or accommodation to use a makerspace. A simple and straightforward example of this would be to measure clearance around design centers, worktables, and equipment. The current Americans with Disabilities Act recommendation for public areas is a clearance of 36 inches.[7] Just as would be done in the other public areas of your library, make sure that the makerspace has room to maneuver to the worktables or machines. The simple act of making the space accessible is akin to a large welcome mat for those of differing abilities. Remove any barriers to entering the space and approaching equipment and staff. As the plans for the makerspace are developed, invite teens to look over the plans. Ask if they can identify any potential barriers to them or their fellow students using the space.

Along with considering different physical abilities, remember to keep in mind potential invisible disabilities. On Priya Ray's website DIYabled, she shares her experiences after sustaining spinal cord and traumatic brain injuries. She writes about what happened when she first tried to access makerspaces and other creative spaces after becoming paralyzed, and the challenges she faced. Her candid evaluations and practical suggestions are an excellent resource for designing makerspaces that are accessible to all. Overall, she says, acknowledgment and attempts go a long way. First, acknowledge when or if someone is having difficulty and offer to help. Second, make honest attempts at accessibility. Do not neglect the actions that you can take to be welcoming to all, including wide aisles or doorways, ramps, if necessary, and friendly staff.[8]

CONCLUSION

Makerspaces are a fantastic way to share technology with your teen library patrons. These makerspaces can be actual physical spaces or mobile units that are accessed periodically. What matters is that they are spaces where teens can come together to express themselves creatively and learn skills that are transferable to future careers. At the heart of public libraries is the mission to provide equal and free education to all. That should include teens, of course, and their need to gain creative problem-solving, digital design, and collaboration skills. All these skills are readily taught in makerspaces.

Libraries wanting to build makerspaces should keep in mind budget, staffing, physical space parameters, continuity of service, and accessibility. The library's budget, staffing allowances, and physical space parameters will define the type of space that is created. No matter how much your budget, makerspace activities and programs are possible. There is a wide range of possibilities, from a cart full of low-tech craft supplies and recyclables to an independent space full of the latest 3D printers and laser cutters. Once the actual space parameters are defined, staff will need to consider the types of programs that are offered and how they best complement the library's mission. Libraries should not neglect to consider the needs of teens with varying abilities or career aspirations.

The most important aspect of a makerspace is to have fun and be creative with your teen patrons.

NOTES

1. "Makerspaces: What Are They?" *Libraries and Maker Culture: A Resource Guide*. Accessed June 23, 2020. https://library-maker-culture.weebly.com/what-are-they.html.

2. Fernández, Covadonga. "The Origins of the Maker Movement." BBVA OpenMind. May 22, 2015. https://www.bbvaopenmind.com/en/technology/innovation/the-origins-of-the-maker-movement/.

3. Fernández. "The Origins of the Maker Movement."

4. UMSI News Service. "Graduate Students Unveil Their Makers Inventions." University of Michigan School of Information. May 5, 2017. https://www.si.umich.edu/about-umsi/news/graduate-students-unveil-their-makers-inventions.

5. At the writing of this book, the Loft serves patrons ages ten to eighteen. For a majority of its history, the Loft served ages twelve to eighteen.

6. The Charlotte Mecklenburg Library employs a consistent pricing structure across all makerspaces for materials consumed for personal projects. If attending an advertised library-led group program, there is no cost for materials for that project. If working one-on-one or in a small group with the advice of staff, there is a small fee for materials.

7. U.S. Access Board. "Chapter 4: Accessible Routes." Americans with Disabilities Act. Accessed June 23, 2020. https://www.access-board.gov/guidelines-and-standards/buildings-and-sites/about-the-ada-standards/ada-standards/chapter-4-accessible-routes.

8. Ray, Priya. DIYabled. Accessed June 23, 2020. http://diyabled.com/.

TEN
Collection Development

Collection development is a foundational component of library services. What follows are recommendations for resources to support both staff development and services to your teen program participants. When developing these collections, it is vitally important to make sure your selections are relevant, engaging, timely, and fresh. Your teen library users may be hesitant to engage with nonfiction selections that are outdated or dry, so we also recommend supplementing recent nonfiction titles with fiction titles that focus on technology.

BOOKS FOR STAFF DEVELOPMENT

The teen-serving librarian must understand the development of the teen mind to serve teens most effectively and compassionately. The teen brain is still developing well into young adulthood. The teens you serve are continuing to process information mostly through the amygdala, a portion of the brain responsible for fear and aggressive reactions, rather than the frontal cortex, the area responsible for logic and reasoning.[1] Beyond understanding the physical science of teen development, library staff should also learn other aspects of teens' development and needs, such as those on the list of core competences developed for library staff by the Young Adult Library Services Association (YALSA). These competencies look at how we are to interact with teens and foster their independence; how to set up welcoming and equitable library spaces and experiences; how to foster cultural competencies, cultural reactions, and community connections; and how to foster continuous learning.[2]

There are several excellent resources for continuing development as a teen-serving librarian. *The Whole Library Handbook: Teen Services* edited by Heather Booth and Karen Jensen does as the title suggests—holistically approaches teen librarianship. The authors cover teen development, best practices for interacting with teens, and how to set up a welcoming and engaging library space. Additionally, the book advises on tracking trends and challenges in working with teens and advocacy for teen library services. For more information about serving teens in libraries, we recommend *Putting Teens First in Library Services: A Road Map* by Linda W. Braun and Shannon Peterson; *Sex, Brains, and Video Games: Information and Inspiration for Youth Services Librarians, 2nd Edition* by Jennifer Burek Pierce; and *Real-World Teen Services* by Jennifer Velásquez. All three of these titles provide a big-picture perspective on teen development, how best to serve teens in a library environment, and information on strategizing for desired outcomes, all through a lens of advocating for your teen library users.

For more details on technology to consider purchasing for your space and how to utilize it with your users, we recommend *How to STEM: Science, Technology, Engineering, and Math Education in Libraries* edited by Vera Gubnitskaia and Carol Smallwood, along with *Technology and the School Library: A Comprehensive Guide for Media Specialists and Other Educators* by Odin L. Jurkowski. Both titles advise on technology purchases for any budget and in any library. Further, *How to STEM* gives suggested program ideas for the recommended technology. If you are stumped as to how to fund all the technology mentioned in these titles, *The ALA Book of Library Grant Money, 9th Edition* edited by Nancy Kalikow Maxwell can help steer you toward grant opportunities. This book lists recurring grant opportunities and is considered the ultimate resource for this topic.

- Booth, Heather, and Karen Jensen, eds. *The Whole Library Handbook: Teen Services.* ALA Editions, 2014.
- Braun, Linda W., and Shannon Peterson. *Putting Teens First in Library Services: A Road Map.* Young Adult Library Services Association (YALSA), 1992.
- Craig, Angela, and Chantell L. McDowell. *Serving At-Risk Teens: Proven Strategies and Programs for Bridging the Gap.* ALA-Neal Schuman, 2013.
- Gubnitskaia, Vera, and Carol Smallwood, eds. *How to STEM: Science, Technology, Engineering, and Math Education in Libraries.* Rowman & Littlefield, 2013.
- Jurkowski, Odin L. *Technology and the School Library: A Comprehensive Guide for Media Specialists and Other Educators.* Rowman & Littlefield, 2017.
- Maxwell, Nancy Kalikow, ed. *The ALA Book of Library Grant Money, 9th Edition.* ALA Editions, 2014.
- Pandora, Cherie P., and Stacey Hayman. *Better Serving Teens through School Library-Public Library Collaborations.* Libraries Unlimited, 2013.
- Pierce, Jennifer Burek. *Sex, Brains, and Video Games: Information and Inspiration for Youth Services Librarians, 2nd Edition.* ALA Editions, 2017.
- Velásquez, Jennifer. *Real-World Teen Services.* ALA Editions, 2015.

BOOKS FOR PROGRAM INSPIRATION

Sharing ideas for programs and outreach can further staff development. Library programs are where you meet, impact, and interact with your teen users. The titles recommended in this section have been tested and shown to be successful with teens and are sure to inspire.

Technology and Literacy: 21st Century Library Programming for Children and Teens by Jennifer Nelson and Keith Braafladt is an excellent book that covers a wide variety of technology-based programs for libraries. The authors connect technology programming to the traditional library service model of literacy instruction with sample program ideas based on Scratch programming, digital storytimes, and technology-based workshops. They advise how to advocate for technology-based programs and evaluate the effectiveness of your programs. This title is our recommendation for a big-picture view of all that can be done with teens and technology in library settings.

If you have or are creating a makerspace in your library, we recommend *The Big Book of Makerspace Projects* by Colleen Graves and Aaron Graves and *63 Ready-to-Use Maker Projects* and *The Makerspace Librarian's Sourcebook*, both edited by Ellyssa Kroski. These three titles are focused on makerspaces and library programs. *The Makerspace Librarian's Sourcebook* advises how to set up your permanent or temporary makerspace, recommends supplies to keep on hand, and gives sample program ideas. *The Big Book of Makerspace*

Projects and *63 Ready-to-Use Maker Projects* offer more program ideas. All three titles cover a range of options for all budgets and space constraints. With these resources, you will be ready to kick off a series of maker programs for your teen library users.

Many libraries provide gaming equipment to patrons during programs or open hours. *Augmented and Virtual Reality in Libraries* edited by Jolanda-Pieta van Arnhem, Christine Elliott, and Marie Rose and *52 Ready-to-Use Gaming Programs for Libraries* edited by Ellyssa Kroski are our recommendations for these types of programs. *Augmented and Virtual Reality in Libraries* gives advice on augmented and virtual reality equipment to consider for your library, best practices for setup, and sample program ideas. *52 Ready-to-Use Gaming Programs for Libraries* provides program ideas and best practices for setup for video game opportunities. Between these two titles, you will be well prepared to offer your teens the gaming programs they desire.

If you plan to take your technology-based programs into your community, we recommend *Your Technology Outreach Adventure* by Erin Berman. This comprehensive book covers the reasons for creating technology outreach, which will give you the foundation you need to advocate for the equipment and time. Additionally, the author provides recommendations for technology purchases and sample programs that cover any variety of budget or staffing limits.

- Berman, Erin. *Your Technology Outreach Adventure: Tools for Human-Centered Problem Solving.* ALA Editions, 2019.
- Graves, Colleen, and Aaron Graves. *The Big Book of Makerspace Projects.* McGraw-Hill Education TAB, 2016.
- Kroski, Ellyssa. *52 Ready-to-Use Gaming Programs for Libraries.* ALA Editions, 2020.
- Kroski, Ellyssa. *63 Ready-to-Use Maker Projects.* ALA Editions, 2017.
- Kroski, Ellyssa. *The Makerspace Librarian's Sourcebook.* ALA Editions, 2017.
- Nelson, Jennifer, and Keith Braafladt. *Technology and Literacy: 21st Century Library Programming for Children and Teens.* ALA Editions, 2011.
- van Arnhem, Jolanda-Pieta; Elliott, Christine, and Marie Rose, eds. *Augmented and Virtual Reality in Libraries.* Rowman & Littlefield, 2018.

BOOKS FOR TEEN LIBRARY PARTICIPANTS

Keep your library well stocked with informative, engaging, and entertaining books for your teen patrons. Keep these titles relevant; teens are not likely to show interest in books, especially nonfiction titles, that have outdated covers or feature any noncontemporary information. The following titles are ones that could be put into a book display or made available at technology-based programs for checkout.

Recommending fiction titles can be difficult, as new books are released regularly. *Ender's Game* by Orson Scott Card and *Little Brother* by Cory Doctorow are two that can always be recommended. They have stood the test of time and continue to entertain and engage teens. Further, the Unearthed series by Amie Kaufman and Meagan Spooner and Dark Intercept series by Julia Keller are two more recently published titles (at the time of this book's publication) that focus on technology and get good reviews from teens and teen librarians. *Ender's Game* incorporates video gaming into a future war scenario; *Little Brother* touches on the use of video surveillance technology in society. Both titles would be good for discussion with a group of teens. The Unearthed series and the Dark Intercept series both focus on teens and space exploration. We recommend reviewing sources such as *Booklist*, *YALS*, and *VOYA* for book reviews as new titles are released.

You will also want to have a selection of relevant and timely nonfiction titles for teens. These books can inspire career exploration or skills and knowledge acquisition. Christy

Peterson's *Into the Deep: Science, Technology, and the Quest to Protect the Ocean* and Reference Point Press's Technology's Impact Series will have teens thinking critically about technology and their futures. Popular Science's *The Popular Science Hacker's Manual* and Rosen Publishing's Getting Creative with Fab Lab series will give teens the foundational skills they need to invent new technology-based products. Should a teen show an interest in using technology in a future career, Rosen Publishing's Coding Your Passion series will give them plenty of ideas and advice on how to pursue their interests. We encourage you to select these books for your teen patrons, display them, and let participants know about them at technology-based programs.

- Card, Orson Scott. *Ender's Game.* Tor Books, 1985.
- Doctorow, Cory. *Little Brother.* Tor Teen, 2008.
- Kaufman, Amie, and Meagan Spooner. Unearthed series. Little, Brown Books for Young Readers, 2018.
- Keller, Julia. Dark Intercept series. Tor Teen, 2017.
- Peterson, Christy. *Into the Deep: Science, Technology, and the Quest to Protect the Ocean.* Twenty-First Century Books, 2020.
- Popular Science. *The Popular Science Hacker's Manual.* Cavendish Square Publishing, 2019.
- Reference Point Press. Technology's Impact Series (*How Artificial Intelligence Will Impact Society; How Drones Will Impact Society; How Nanotechnology Will Impact Society; How Self-Driving Cars Will Impact Society; How 3D Printing Will Impact Society; How Virtual Reality Will Impact Society*). Reference Point Press, 2018.
- Rosen Publishing. Coding Your Passion series (*Using Computer Science in High-Tech Criminal Justice Careers; Using Computer Science in Financial Technology Careers; Using Computer Science in High-Tech Health and Wellness Careers; Using Computer Science in Digital Music Careers; Using Computer Science in Online Retail Careers; Using Computer Science in Digital Gaming Careers*). Rosen Publishing, 2018.
- Rosen Publishing. Getting Creative with Fab Lab series (*Creating with 3D Printers; Creating with 3D Scanners; Creating with Laser Cutters and Engravers; Creating with Milling Machines; Creating with Digital Sewing Machines; Creating with Vinyl Cutters*). Rosen Publishing, 2017.

FURTHER RESOURCES

Beyond books, we would like to recommend a few other resources for you to consider reading. Earlier in this book, we discussed the economic opportunity research from Harvard. The full report by Raj Chetty and additional tools are available at the Opportunity Insights website at opportunityinsights.org. The research gives insights into how your area may be doing in terms of economic mobility, ideas for how your library can support improvements, and facts to use to advocate for technology-based programs.

Two publications regularly give program ideas and book reviews: *YALS* and *VOYA*. *YALS* is delivered to members of YALSA, the Young Adult Library Services Association, and *VOYA* (*Voice of Youth Advocates*) can be subscribed to directly. Your library may help pay for professional organizations or professional development publications, and your supervisor or director can tell you how to apply for those funds.

The magazines *Make:* and *Popular Science* are worth consideration. The project ideas in each issue will inspire you and your teen patrons, and the technology reviews can help inform your future technology purchases.

CONCLUSION

Books and magazines can support your professional development and help you make informed decisions on programs and technology purchases. The titles listed in this chapter will inspire you and your teens to create, learn, and grow. We further encourage you to read book review publications and continue to add to your technology-based collection.

NOTES

1. American Academy of Child and Adolescent Psychiatry. "Teen Brain: Behavior, Problem Solving, and Decision Making." September 2016. https://www.aacap.org/AACAP/Families_and_Youth/Facts_for_Families/FFF-Guide/The-Teen-Brain-Behavior-Problem-Solving-and-Decision-Making-095.aspx.
2. YALSA. "Teen Services Competencies for Library Staff." July 9, 2019. http://www.ala.org/yalsa/guidelines/yacompetencies.

ELEVEN
Sample Technology Programs

BOARD GAME DESIGN

Related Topics: Gaming
Intended Audience: Preteens, Teens
Estimated Length of Time for Program: 60 minutes. This program can also be turned into a short series, depending on how you want to expand or contract it. They can develop their games extensively and playtest them several times. Or they can just be introduced to some basic concepts and resources for board game design as a new approach the next time they play.

Supplies Needed

- A variety of drawing utensils (pens, pencils, erasers, markers, colored pencils, crayons)
- A variety of paper (construction, colored, magazine, cardstock, index cards, or even easel paper)
- Scissors, rulers, glue
- Playing pieces that can be made on the 3D printer or random bits from a thrift store
- Random household objects (coffee beans, glass beads, miniatures, feathers, candy)
- Examples of both familiar and unfamiliar board games for kids

Instructions for Program

As many board games exist, there are equally as many ways to approach this program. If you have a board gaming store in your community, you may want to reach out to them to speak on their knowledge of new board games, how they would go about game design, or even what made them follow their passion for a career.

Another suggestion to start the program is to have the youth do "speed dating" with various board games set up throughout the programming space. Have them fill out existing sheets that ask what they like/do not like about the game, the obstacles, and what they might change in designing the game. They can then share their thoughts with the larger group. They can also focus on other popular games such as kickball, tag, and basketball to apply the same criteria. The goal is to get them to think of themselves as creators and editors of an experience.

Next, you may want to have them define common terms of a game such as the story, setting, characters, or at least those areas that you will have them cover when they design their own game. A gaming expert or a meet-up group can be helpful, virtually or recorded. Game design is also a scout badge, so you might consider reaching out to scouting groups to see if anyone would be willing to present their findings. Rule books can also be great resources for defining terms.

One way that may connect quickly with the audience (rather than asking them to start from a blank piece of paper to design their game) is to have them work in small groups and choose a theme. They need to pick up objects from a table that are provided and include them in their game. After an amount of time has passed, they can put it in a playable format, allowing them to present the idea to the group. Each group will get a few minutes to play the game and suggest one rule they would change and why. They will have the opportunity to present this to the group that developed the game.

Intended Outcome

Participants will learn a different approach to gameplay; they will learn how to be creators and not just consumers. They can be exposed to the career aspect of selling and creating board games. They will learn how to give feedback and receive it as well.

Resources

International Games Week with the American Library Association: https://games.ala.org/igw_promos/

Game Jam (YALSA Programming HQ): http://hq.yalsa.net/programs/3759/game-jam-playing-making-games

DRY ICE BUBBLE GENERATOR

Related Topics: Tech without Tech, Chemistry
Intended Audience: Preteens, Teens, Young Adults
Estimated Length of Time for Program: 45 minutes
Supplies Needed

- Empty and dry disinfectant wipes containers
- Rubber tubing
- Plastic cups
- Duct tape
- Dry ice
- Hot water
- Scissors
- Paint or permanent markers (optional)
- Liquid dish soap

Instructions for Program

Optional: Begin by inviting participants to decorate their empty containers.

Instruct each participant to cut a small hole on the side of their container, about half an inch to an inch below the container's lid. Help if needed.

Instruct each participant to cut a small hole in the center of the bottom of their plastic cup.

Give each participant a length of rubber tubing approximately 18 inches long. Instruct participants to insert one end into the hole in their container and the other end into the bottom of their cup. Secure both ends with duct tape to create a seal.

Place a small (palm-sized or slightly smaller) piece of dry ice in each bubble generator. Lightly dip the rim of the plastic cup into soapy water. Add half a cup of hot water to each bubble generator and close the top.

The resulting mist will leave the bubble generator through the rubber tubing. As it passes through the cup, bubbles will form that have mist inside. The bubble generators can be continually refilled with fresh dry ice and hot water.

Intended Outcome

Participants will learn about states of matter and surface tension.

GAME DESIGN WITH BLOXELS

Related Topics: Gaming
Intended Audience: Preteens, Teens
Estimated Length of Time for Program: 60 minutes (Though if you want to create a more involved game and your audience lends itself to showing up multiple times, this could be run as a series program where they have a set of tasks they complete each session.)

Supplies Needed

- Tablet (one per three youth) or a tablet connected to a projector
- Free Bloxels app
- Wi-Fi
- Bloxels Builder platform (starts at $23 each at various stores). See other kits available for classrooms, larger groups, etc., at https://store.bloxelsbuilder.com/. Devices that work with Bloxels include iOS, Android, Kindle, and Chromebook. For more FAQs, consult the Bloxels education page: https://edu.bloxelsbuilder.com/.

Instructions for Program

Have an icebreaker planned, especially if the participants do not know one another and will need to pair up. After the icebreaker, initiate a discussion about game design and gameplay. Youth can share which games they play and why. They can talk about any experience with a game design they might have had.

Divide youth up into small groups, depending on the number of resources you have. If just using one large screen that is projecting a tablet, the teens can take turns contributing to various aspects of the game. If they are in small groups, have them start playing some of the games on the Bloxels Arcade available for 5 to 10 minutes. They can be invited back to regroup and critique their experience. What did they like, or what would they have done differently as a creator?

Give a brief overview of where teens can find access to Bloxels tutorials (http://www.bloxelsbuilder.com/tutorials) if they want to gather more information on how to do things. Many teens will likely want to jump in and try something rather than spending a lot of time reading the manual, but give them the option!

It can be helpful to give them a guide or a legend for what the block types mean (though many are intuitive, such as the blue blocks are for liquid or water). Participants can review the website http://www.bloxelsbuilder.com/blocktypes, or you may want to create a quick handout. If the youth are not game players, they may need help from one another to understand what terms like "power up" mean.

Then give them tasks. Have them create at least one character, a level, and several obstacles to get through. Allow them to play one another's games, respectfully critique, and even make changes if time allows. Spend some time in conversation about what it means to give helpful feedback to someone as opposed to insulting putdowns with no solutions offered. Having a simple handout that asks them to name three things they liked about the game and one thing they might change can get them started.

While you don't have to be an expert at Bloxels yourself, at least be familiar with several of the tutorials and set up an account to complete the tasks you are asking the youth to do. If you want a backup for some assurance, invite a gamer willing to volunteer and help troubleshoot. Feel free to keep your attendance numbers low if you wish to pilot the program in what might feel like a safer way to get your bearings.

Intended Outcome

Participants will learn to gain some basic coding skills, give and accept feedback, and revise a project. This hobby or interest may grow into a career they want to pursue!

GETTING STARTED: ONLINE RESEARCH

Related Topics: Career Readiness & Exploration, Educational Success
Intended Audience: Preteens, Teens, Young Adults
Estimated Length of Time for Program: 60 to 90 minutes
Supplies Needed

- Laptop or internet PC for each participant
- Projector with a laptop for presenting staff

Instructions for Program

Preparation: Compile a list of resources and databases that you will cover in the program and create either a handout or brochure. Plan to highlight those resources that are of the most use to teens in their academic pursuits. These include your library's research database for articles and excerpts and any teen health, biographical, career exploration, and test preparation resources.

Open the program by inviting participants to share what they hope to learn. Write these down so that you can answer throughout the program. Share why verified resources are important when seeking information. Show the examples of Google searches for "Martin Luther King Jr." (often there are opinion sites not aligned with his values among the top hits) or "Pacific Northwest Tree Octopus" (not a real creature, but the top hit is a website full of information on it). Have all the participants search for the same term or phrase and share their top five results. The results will vary, and this illustrates that your activity on the web can skew results.

Next, you will work through demonstrating each of the resources that you selected to highlight. Invite the participants to explore the resources along with you. Ask questions and challenge the participants to find the answers within the resources.

At the end of the program, allow time for participants to ask questions. Remind participants that all featured resources are listed in the brochure or on the handout that you have distributed. Let participants know of any future programs or further resources at your library that they can use.

Intended Outcome

Participants will become familiar with library resources and online research techniques. Participants will further their educational success and career readiness.

GUY TALK: TECHNOLOGY EDITION

Related Topics: Tech without Tech, Discussion
Intended Audience: Preteens, Teens, Young Adults
Estimated Length of Time for Program: 45 minutes
Supplies Needed

- Snacks (optional)

Instructions for Program

Preparation: Become familiar with a current technology issue or event.

Guy Talk programs are informal and can take place in a program room or the public space. Snacks are recommended but optional.

First, invite participating teens to grab a snack, if providing, and take a seat. Share that this is a discussion program and ask participants to respect each other, respect the space, and respect themselves. Open by sharing the topic or current event that you have investigated. Briefly describe the issue or development, including both positives and detractors.

Open the floor for comments. Invite all participants to share their initial reactions. Invite participants to share any further information they have heard. Encourage discussion and debate regarding the issue itself or the source of information. Continually encourage participants to remain respectful of one another while sharing.

Here are some examples of topics from 2019. For your program, you will want to use a current event or issue.

- Facebook and privacy
- Facial recognition software used for security
- Accelerated growth of the Internet of Things
- Branding yourself on social media

Intended Outcome

Participants will become more aware of the impact technology can have on the world and current events.

HOUR OF CODE

Related Topics: Career Readiness and Exploration, Educational Success
Intended Audience: Preteens
Estimated Length of Time for Program: 90 minutes
Supplies Needed

- Laptop or internet PC for each participant

Instructions for Program

Preparation: Library staff member will turn on each laptop or internet PC and navigate to Hour of Code website: http://www.hourofcode.com.

At the start of the program, introduce coding as a language and explain its importance to educational success and future career possibilities. Explain that today the group will together explore coding through a series of games and videos.

Have all participants select the same challenge. Explain that it is not a race, that the staff is present to assist and help keep everyone moving forward together. In between each two or three challenges, there will be a short video that the group can view at the same time.

As students complete challenges, remain available for questions or assistance. Periodically invite students to share solutions. The program is intended to be completed in an hour but may take a little longer if you work with a larger group.

Intended Outcome

Participants will receive a broad introduction to coding and learn how this connects to their current educational success and future career success.

MEET A PROFESSIONAL

Related Topics: Career Readiness & Exploration
Intended Audience: Preteens, Teens, Young Adults
Estimated Length of Time for Program: 45 to 60 minutes
Supplies Needed

- Projector (optional)
- Snacks (optional)

Instructions for Program

Preparation: Recruit a community member working in a technology-related career to present at your library, based on teen recommendations or interests. Let the professional know what you expect in the number of teen attendees, atmosphere, and presentation length. Recommended: a 30-minute presentation followed by time for questions from participants. You can also encourage the professional to bring hands-on objects to illustrate their work, allow the teens to have a tangible aspect of participation, and provide giveaways from their company.

As participants enter, encourage them to grab snacks if providing. To start the program, introduce the professional and give their background and job title. State that they are there to share information about their job with the participants and encourage questions.

The visiting professional should share their current job title, what their work entails, what a typical workday looks like, what other jobs they have held in the same field or company, and what educational or training background was required to join their career.

During the program, the professional can pass around any tangibles they brought to interact with the participants.

After the program, allow time for questions from the participants. Have a prepared list of questions ready to start off this segment in case no teens step forward.

A further consideration: library staff can recruit several technology professionals to come speak at their library, creating a program series over a few months.

Intended Outcome

Participants will become familiar with technology-based careers that they may not have previously considered.

PAPER CIRCUITS

Related Topics: Tech without Tech, Electricity
Intended Audience: Teens, Young Adults
Estimated Length of Time for Program: 45 minutes
Supplies Needed

- Cardstock paper
- Copper tape
- Coin cell batteries
- Small LED lights
- Markers or colored pencils

Instructions for Program

Begin by explaining electrical circuits to participants. Electricity must go from one side of the coin cell battery to the other to create a current. Anything (such as an LED light) placed in between the flow from one side to the other must also conduct electricity.

Show participants how to affix an LED and a coin cell battery to a sheet of cardstock and create a circuit using the copper tape. Use copper tape to connect the longer LED leg (the positive one) to the battery's negative (-) side. Repeat for connecting the shorter LED leg (the negative one) to the battery's positive (+) side. The light will be lit.

Next, demonstrate how a circuit could be created that is only completed when the paper is folded. When the paper is unfolded, the light goes out.

Invite the participants to try creating both kinds of circuits. Move about the room, assisting as needed.

Invite the participants to create a greeting card that incorporates light or challenge them to create a design that includes more than one LED.

At the program conclusion, invite participants to share their work with the group and share anything they learned during creation.

Intended Outcome

Participants will learn about electrical circuits.

SQUISHY CIRCUITS

Related Topics: Tech without Tech, Electronics
Intended Audience: Preteens, Teens
Estimated Length of Time for Program: 60 minutes
Supplies Needed

- Flour

- Salt
- Cream of tartar
- Water
- Vegetable oil
- Food coloring
- Sugar
- Distilled water
- Coin cell batteries
- Insulated wires with exposed ends
- Small LED lights

Instructions for Program

Optional Preparation: Create batches of insulating and conductive dough before the program. If you do this, skip the next step in the instructions. Otherwise, simply gather all materials and continue to the next step.

Participants begin by making the insulating and the conductive dough. Depending on the skill level and size of the group, you can direct the group to do one of these options:

- Work together as a group to make both types of dough.
- Split into two groups to each make one type of dough.
- Split into multiple small groups to each make both types of dough.
- Split into multiple small groups to each make one type of dough.

In the end, you should facilitate the sharing of dough among participants or groups so that everyone has access to both conductive and insulating dough.

Instructions for Making Conductive Dough: Mix 1½ cups flour, ¼ cup salt, 1 tablespoon cream of tartar, 1 cup water, 2 tablespoons vegetable oil, and food coloring together to form a dough. Add small amounts of flour, if too wet, or water, if too dry.

Instructions for Making Insulating Dough: Mix 1½ cups flour, ½ cup sugar, 3 tablespoons vegetable oil, ½ cup distilled water, and food coloring together to form a dough. Add small amounts of flour, if too wet, or distilled water, if too dry. Food coloring used should be a different color from the conductive dough.

Explain to participants that the conductive dough allows electrical current to move through it. The insulating dough stops the electrical current that tries to enter it. Explain that electricity needs to make a complete circuit to function. Both the (+) and (-) sides of the batteries must be connected to their creations for electrical current to run through.

Demonstrate by taking a bit of conductive dough and dividing it into two pieces. Roll into a rough ball. Take an LED light and bend the legs outward. Insert one leg into each ball of dough, keeping the balls from touching. Connect one ball to the (+) side of the battery using an insulated wire. Connect the other ball to the (-) side of the battery using insulated wire. The current will run from one side of the battery, through the first ball, out through the LED leg, back down the other LED leg, into the other ball, and back to the other side of the battery, causing the LED to light up.

Demonstrate what happens when the current can skip the LED by placing the balls next to each other, touching. The LED no longer lights up. Demonstrate what happens when you add a piece of insulating dough between the two balls: even though all dough is now touching, the LED lights up again because the connection is broken between the two balls of conductive dough.

Challenge participants to build with the dough and LEDs. In case creativity is short, have a list of suggestions ready, such as rockets with lights at the nose, a flower with a lit center, a dinosaur with lit spikes down its back, and more.

After the program, ask participants to share their creations with the group, explain what they have made, and share anything they have learned.

Intended Outcome

Participants will learn about electricity and electrical currents.

TECH LIT BOOK DISCUSSION

Related Topics: Tech without Tech, Literacy
Intended Audience: Preteens, Teens, Young Adults
Estimated Length of Time for Program: 60 minutes
Supplies Needed

- Snacks (optional)

Instructions for Program

Preparation: Become familiar with the chosen title and develop a list of questions for discussion in the group. Set out snacks if providing.

A tech lit book discussion will run similarly to most other book clubs. It can be a single event or a recurring book club. Books chosen for discussion should include technology as a major device and appeal to young adults. The discussion should have questions relating to technology in the title.

During the program, the staff member or teen moderator should ensure that all participants can share if they would like.

The following are some suggested titles for this program. There are others continually being released.

- *The Drowned Cities* by Paolo Bacigalupi
- *Ender's Game* by Orson Scott Card
- *Ready Player One* by Ernest Cline
- *In Real Life* by Cory Doctorow
- *Little Brother* by Cory Doctorow
- *Willful Machines* by Tim Floreen
- *Cinder* by Marissa Meyer
- *Want* by Cindy Pon
- *Starters* by Lissa Price
- *The Body Electric* by Beth Revis

Intended Outcome

Participants will become more aware of the impact technology can have upon a story, whether it is their story or a story in a novel.

TECHNOLOGY TUTORING FOR SENIORS

Related Topics: Aligning with Library Mission
Intended Audience: Teens, Young Adults, Senior Adults
Estimated Length of Time for Program: 30 to 60 minutes, occurring on a regular schedule

Supplies Needed

- Optional: library-owned ereaders, laptops, or internet PCs

Instructions for Program

Preparation: Teen volunteers will be recruited for the program and trained in basic customer-service skills. Their technology skills are assessed. Senior adults contact the library to register for the program to receive one-on-one assistance with their technology, such as a laptop, software, internet program, or electronic reader. Senior adults are matched with a teen with the necessary skills or knowledge for one-on-one assistance.

On the day of the program, the room should be set up with tables and pairs of chairs for the teens and senior adults. If possible and applicable, teens should be provided with library devices to use in the demonstration.

Intended Outcome

Senior adults will feel more comfortable and confident using technology. Teens will make connections with older adults, strengthening the community.

VIRTUAL DUNGEONS & DRAGONS WITH THE LIBRARY

Related Topics: Gaming
Intended Audience: Preteens, Teens
Estimated Length of Time for Program: 1 to 2 hours
Supplies Needed

- Create an account on Roll20
- Basic D&D rules (https://dnd.wizards.com/articles/features/basicrules)
- Roll20 builds in what they call the Compendium into all D&D 5th Edition games played through their site. Most of the basic information for players and Dungeon Masters (DMs) can be found in this Compendium, and it is integrated into the character sheets created through the site and any journal entries the DM creates for the game.
- Dice
- Polyhedral Dice, 7-Piece Set (d4, d6, d8, d10, d%, d12, d20)
- Roll20 comes with 3D Dice
- D&D cheat sheets (http://bit.ly/DnDCheatSheets)
- These sheets are notes on how to play for players and new DMs (action reminders, dice type, etc.)
- Notebook and pencil for writing down notes

Instructions for Program

Introduction: "Welcome to Virtual Dewey and Dragons/Dungeons and Dragons for Teens/Dungeons and Dragons for Tweens. Today we will all be participating in a fantasy adventure to work together to tell a tale of heroism and adventure. I will be your Dungeon Master and act as your guide during this fantasy role-playing game. Let the adventure begin!"

Closing: "Well done, adventurers! If you would like to continue this adventure, please be on the lookout for our next scheduled session. In the meantime, check out some of the materials in our collection to help you understand the game better and help you become a Dungeon Master and run your games."

Cost: $0 to $50

Dungeon Master Basics:

The Dungeon Master (DM) has a special role in the Dungeons & Dragons game.

The DM is a referee. When it is not clear what ought to happen next, the DM decides how to apply the rules and keep the story going.

The DM is a narrator. The DM sets the story's pace and presents the various challenges and encounters the players must overcome. The DM is the players' interface to the D&D world and the one who reads (and sometimes also writes) the adventure and describes what happens in response to the characters' actions.

The DM plays monsters. The DM plays the monsters and villains the adventurers battle against, choosing their actions and rolling dice for their attacks. The DM also plays the part of all the other characters the players meet during their adventures, like the prisoner in the goblin lair or the town's innkeeper.

Although the DM controls the monsters and villains in the adventure, the relationship between the players and the DM is not adversarial. The DM's job is to challenge the characters with exciting encounters and tests, keep the game moving, and apply the rules fairly. The most important thing to remember about being a good DM is that the rules are a tool to help you have a good time. The rules are not in charge. You are the DM. You oversee the game. Guide the play experience and the use of the rules so that everybody has fun.

Rules to Game By: As the Dungeon Master, you are the final authority for rules, questions, or disputes during the game. Here are some guidelines to help you arbitrate issues as they come up:

When in doubt, make it up! It is better to keep the game moving than to get bogged down in the rules.

It is not a competition. The DM is not competing against the player characters. You are there to run the monsters, referee the rules, and keep the story moving.

It is a shared story. It is the group's story, so let the players contribute to the outcome through their characters' actions. Dungeons & Dragons is about imagination and coming together to tell a story as a group. Let the players participate in the storytelling.

Be consistent. If you decide that a rule works a certain way in one session, make sure it works that way the next time it comes into play.

Involve everyone. Make sure everyone is involved. Ensure every character has a chance to shine. If some players are reluctant to speak up, remember to ask them what their characters are doing.

Be fair. Use your powers as Dungeon Master only for good. Treat the rules and the players fairly and impartially.

Pay attention. Make sure you look around the table occasionally to see if the game is going well. If everyone seems to be having fun, relax and keep going. If the fun is waning, it might be time for a break, or you can try to liven things up.

Procedure:

- Ensure your players have created a Roll20 account.
- Email them a link to your campaign (players can only log in to a campaign with an invitation link; Roll20 sessions are secure).
- Greet players and begin the program by giving them an overview of D&D and how it is played.
- Discuss Safety Tools for your sessions (see Resources, at the end of the section).

- Play D&D using the provided adventure. Available for free as part of a "Stay at Home, Play at Home" effort in cooperation with Wizards of the Coast, https://marketplace.roll20.net/browse/module/40/the-masters-vault.
- Encourage the players to make a backstory for their character.
- Players can pick from premade characters or create their level-1 character.
    - Human Cleric
    - Elf Wizard
    - Halfling Rogue
    - Dwarf Fighter
    - Tiefling Bard
    - Dragonborn Paladin
- The Journal is divided into four acts outlined in the adventure, which take the players through several different dungeons and areas around the Merriam Vale. Each act has a lengthy overview that outlines everything that happens (or should happen). Individual areas and dungeons are given separate sections, most with annotated maps.

Player Basics:

Tool Box: (In order) Pan or Zoom tool, Drawing Shape, Zoom, Snapping or Measuring Tool, Dice Roller, and Advanced Roll. Wiki help icon.

Chat and Journal Icon: Here you will find your character sheet and can chat with your fellow players and Dungeon Master (DM) as well as look at any characters or material handouts the DM sends you.

Intended Outcome

Dungeons and Dragons (D&D) is a cooperative game of community storytelling. A group of people gathers to tell a story where the players are the main characters (player characters, or PCs). The story can involve questing for treasure, battling deadly foes, pulling off daring rescues or heists, surviving courtly intrigue or small-town politics, and so much more. One person takes the role of Dungeon Master (DM), who fills multiple roles. They are the narrator and the cast of non-player characters (NPCs), with whom the PCs interact throughout their tales.

During the game, players encounter different situations that encourage critical thinking, communication, math skills, public speaking, collaborative problem-solving, and imagination. The DM sets a scene. The players decide what they want to do to progress the story. The DM describes how those choices turn out or affect the story at large. Many actions that both the PCs and the DM take are resolved "randomly" by rolling dice. Unlike many games, there are no "winners" in D&D. The main goal, again, is for the DM and the players to create an interesting and entertaining story together.

As part of a "Stay at Home, Play at Home" effort in cooperation with Wizards of the Coast (WotC) and other TTRPG (tabletop role-playing game) creators, Roll20 virtual tabletop site has released many digital assets to make it easier to connect players and Dungeon Masters (DMs) during the pandemic. Many of these assets are complete adventures, while others include prompts, guides, or sneak peeks at larger works that can be purchased through the site, available for a limited time.

WotC has also launched its Digital Club Support Program, which includes all the official digital sourcebooks published to date on their website D&DBeyond. This toolkit allows the DM to have all their sources readily available online for easy reference. This toolkit will allow DMs free access to multiple resources that would normally cost a *lot* of money. This kit is available for "organizer[s] representing an enrichment organization within the U.S. or Canada, such as a school, library, community center, scout troop."

Possibilities for online play other than Roll20 include the use of "Theatre of the Mind." This type of play does not rely on props, maps, and handouts. The game/story is played out entirely by the description of actions and reactions and setting the scenes verbally. To play this way, the players and DM still need to connect virtually. This can be accomplished by setting up a dedicated, private Discord chat server to which only the program members are invited. Discord is a popular chat program that many teens already use to communicate, collaborate, and interact with creators of various online content and can be accessed via computer, tablet, or phone. The software includes text, audio, and video chat capabilities. It also has an integrated dice-rolling bot and the capacity to import character sheets created on D&DBeyond or Google Sheets.

You can also explore the many worlds of D&D through any of hundreds of novels, as well as engaging board games and immersive video games. All these stories are part of D&D.

Resources

D&D Basic Rules: https://bit.ly/2HVXXwo
16 Pregenerated Characters: http://www.squaremans.com/PreGens.zip
Safety Tools Discussion: https://youtu.be/yFDbukm5zGI
Roll20 Virtual TableTop for D&D Adventures: https://roll20.net/welcome
Available for free as part of a "Stay at Home, Play at Home" effort in cooperation with Wizards of the Coast: https://marketplace.roll20.net/browse/module/40/the-masters-vault
Roll20 Crash Course: https://roll20.zendesk.com/hc/en-us/articles/360039223834-Roll20-Crash-Course
Tutorial Time, Roll20 Games Master Series: https://youtu.be/djT-5NN5kd0
Roll20 GM Overview, Learn the Basics! https://youtu.be/9ekQ3uLLqL8
Roll20 Tips: https://www.youtube.com/playlist?list=PLTj75n3v9eTnOLIjBpzL7N5C9yysxUddJ
You can find a list of D&D related materials located in the CML system here: http://bit.ly/DeweyandDragonsList
Meet the Roll20 Charactermancer: How to Build and Play a Tabletop Character in Minutes: https://youtu.be/xfxV1GobyQ8
How to Play D&D Online, Roll20 Tutorial: https://youtu.be/0K2VORvNapM

More Fun Resources

Beginning Level Adventures: http://www.dndadventure.com/html/adventures/adv1.html
Matthew Colville, Running the Game (http://bit.ly/2ZyDsgs). Fantastic introduction to playing Dungeons & Dragons as a DM. Takes you step-by-step in running a game and engaging players. Highly recommended for anyone who wants to run a game of Dungeons & Dragons.
Critical Role: Handbooker Helper (http://bit.ly/2Pc1hGX). Excellent videos about the ins and outs of the Player's Handbook, from the use of dice to proficiencies to ability checks.
The Adventure Zone Podcast (https://spoti.fi/2L0I9rv). Actual play podcast. Get a feel how a game of D&D is run. Depicts on-the-fly group storytelling. WARNING: Adult language.

Return of the Lazy Dungeon Master (https://amzn.to/2LbjfnT). If you plan on making your own D&D sessions or campaigns in the future, this is an excellent source that streamlines the process for creating an adventure.

—Created by Jamey Rorie, Chris Spradlin, and Laura Vallejo with the Charlotte Mecklenburg Library

Index

3D printer, 14, 32, 41, 65, 69–72, 74, 76

academic libraries, 17, 28
ALA. *See* American Library Association
Amazon, 50
American Library Association (ALA), 6, 21, 38, 39
Americans with Disabilities Act, 75
Apple, 44
Arduino, 73
augmented reality, 3
Autodesk, 74

Beaverton City Library (Oregon), 27, 32
Belgrade Community Library (Montana), 6
Bernier, Anthony, 16
Birmingham (Alabama), 47, 48
Bloxels, 7, 8
blue screen, 8, 42, 43, 71
Booklist, 79
Boston (Massachusetts), 48
Boston Public Library (Massachusetts), 48
budget, 5, 19–21, 22, 23, 25, 70, 76, 79

careers, 30, 38, 42, 47, 48, 51, 52, 53, 71, 79
Carvey, 71, 72
Census Report, 57
Charleston County Public Library (South Carolina), 27
Charlotte (North Carolina), 7, 27, 28, 29, 30, 31, 47, 49–50, 53, 71
Charlotte Mecklenburg Library (North Carolina), 7, 17, 27, 29, 47, 53, 71
Cincinnati Public Library (Ohio), 39
Cleveland Public Library (Ohio), 27
CNC router, 69
Code-a-Pillars, 32
coding 4, 6, 52
college, 3, 15, 29, 38, 47, 49
computer(s), 3, 6–9, 13–14, 32, 33, 39, 42, 48, 49, 56, 61, 69, 71, 72
Connected Learning, 40
COVID, 13, 14, 16, 17, 24, 38, 39, 56
Craig, Angela, 61
Cricut 7, 66
crocheting, 65
Culatta, Richard, 63

Cuyahoga County Public Library (Ohio), 48

Dashes, 32
Data & Society Institute, 49
Developmental Assets Framework, 40
digital citizens(hip), 32, 49, 63
diversity, 37
DIYabled, 75
Dollar General Summer Learning Grant, 53
dry ice bubble generator, 67, 84
Doctorow, Cory, 62
Dungeons & Dragons, 17

E2D. *See* Eliminate the Digital Divide
ebooks, 5, 17
Eliminate the Digital Divide (E2D), 56
endowment, 21, 22
entrepreneur, 39, 73
equity, 37
ereaders 5
Etsy, 69

Fab Lab, 69
Facebook, 5, 17, 32, 49, 50
filmmaking, 8, 41
Fontaine, Claire, 49
Friends of the Library, 19, 21–23, 25

gaming, 3, 4, 6, 9, 16, 17, 32, 42, 47, 52, 79
GarageBand, 42, 43, 44
Ginsberg, Sharona, 69
Google, 6, 50, 73
grant, 6, 7, 8, 19–20, 23–25, 37, 40, 56, 78
Great Pacific Northwest Tree Octopus, 50
Greenville County Library, 27, 33
Guy Talk, 62

Harvard, 47, 57, 80
Huntersville (North Carolina), 72

I AM Not the MEdia, 49
I Can Animate, 44
Idea Box, 53, 71, 73, 74
iMac, 42
ImaginOn, 8, 30, 71, 72, 73
IMLS. *See* Institute of Museum and Library Services

iMovie, 42–44
inclusion, 15, 27, 31, 37, 39, 66, 75
inclusive. *See* inclusion
Inclusivity. *See* inclusion
Instagram, 4, 5, 14, 16, 17
Institute of Museum and Library Services (IMLS), 20
Instructables.com, 44
International Society for Technology in Education, 63
internet, 4, 5, 16, 32, 49–50, 51, 61, 65, 67
internship, 30, 48, 51, 52, 53, 56
iPad(s), 7, 8, 18, 42, 44
iPhone, 18, 62

Kahoot!, 50
Klinenberg, Eric, 32
knitting, 65

laser cutter, 65, 69, 70, 71, 76
Leading on Opportunity, 47
LeBret, Becky, 66
LEGO Robotics, 6
library card, 9, 17, 39, 43
Library Services and Technology Act (LSTA), 7, 8, 20
LinkedIn, 38
littleBits, 7
Little Brother, 62, 79, 80
Loft, 53, 71, 72
LSTA. *See* Library Services and Technology Act
Lynda.com, 43, 44

Make:, 66, 69, 80
MakerBot, 74
Maker Faire, 69
Maker Movement, 69
makerspace, 3, 7, 14, 15, 30, 32, 33, 41, 48, 52–53, 61, 65–67, 69–76, 78
Makey Makey, 73
McDonald's, 48
McDowell, Chantell L., 61
mentor, 37–41
mentorship. *See* mentor
mentoring. *See* mentor
Messy Makerspace, 53, 72, 73
Microsoft Word, 49
MIDI-enabled keyboard, 42
MIT (Massachusetts Institute of Technology), 69
mobile devices, 5, 7, 50, 61, 62, 65
Multnomah Public Library (Oregon), 20
music, 4, 8, 15, 42, 71

North County Regional Library (Charlotte, North Carolina), 72

Oculus Go, 7
Opportunity Insights, 80
Organization for Economic Co-operation and Development, 49
origami, 67
Ozobots, 7, 32

Pack Memorial Library (North Carolina), 5
pandemic. *See* COVID
paper circuits, 66, 67, 89
paper crafts, 65
partnership(s), 13, 14, 24, 40, 55, 56, 57
Pendergrass, Jay, 62
Penn State University, 32
Pew Research, 63
podcast, 72
Popular Science, 80
professional development, 38
programming: guidelines, 28, 29, 33, 40–42, 43, 47, 48, 49, 50, 51, 52, 56, 61, 64, 67, 70, 71, 73–76, 78, 78–79, 79; outreach, 16, 17, 32, 50, 61–62, 64–65, 67, 78, 79; virtual, 13, 14, 16, 16–18
Public Library Association/PLA, 39

Quizlet, 50

Ray, Priya, 75
ReadyANIMATOR, 42, 44, 71
recording booth, 42, 71
research database, 49, 50, 51
Richland County (South Carolina), 70
robotics, 14, 24, 37, 42

San Francisco (California), 62
San Mateo (California), 69
school libraries, 17, 28
Scratch, 78
screen printing, 72
Search Institute, 40
Serving At-Risk Teens: Proven Strategies and Programs for Bridging the Gap, 61
sewing machine(s), 42, 44, 53, 71
Shusterman, Neal, 62
Silhouette die-cut machine, 42
SkillPop, 38
Snapchat, 5
social justice, 16
social media, 4, 5, 14, 17, 31, 32, 49–50, 63
sound booth, 8
SouthPark Regional Library (Charlotte, North Carolina), 71, 72, 73
Spartanburg County Public Library (South Carolina), 7
Sphero robot. *See* Sphero

Sphero(s), 7, 14, 29
Squishy Circuits, 64, 67, 89
stop motion animation, 43, 44, 71
Stop Motion Studio, 42, 44
Studio i, 41–44, 71, 72
summer reading, 7, 56
summer slide, 29
SUNY Oswego, 69
survey, 39, 65

Thingiverse, 74
Tinkercad, 74

Uglies, 62
University of Alabama, 53
University of California Berkley, 47, 51, 52, 57
Unwind, 62

Veescope Live, 42, 44
video game. *See* gaming

vinyl cutter, 41, 53, 71, 72
virtual reality, 79
vocational, 30
VolunTeen(s), 42–43
volunteer(ing), 13, 30, 31, 33, 41–42, 48, 52, 70, 71, 75
Voice of Youth Advocates (VOYA), 79, 80
VOYA. *See Voice of Youth Advocates*

Westerfeld, Scott, 62
woodworking, 70, 71

YALS. *See Young Adult Library Services*
YALSA. *See* Young Adult Library Services Association
Young Adult Library Services (YALS), 79, 80
Young Adult Library Services Association (YALSA), 13, 38, 40, 77, 80

Zuckerberg, Mark, 49

About the Authors

Kelly Nicole Czarnecki completed her Master of Science in 2002 and Master of Education in 2001 at the University of Illinois Champaign-Urbana. She worked at the Bloomington Public Library in Illinois for four years as the young adult services librarian. Czarnecki started at the Charlotte Mecklenburg Library at the ImaginOn branch in the early 2000s as the teen librarian and then the Teen Loft manager, where she presently works. Czarnecki also has more than twenty years' experience in working with persons experiencing homelessness who are sheltered. She has contributed extensively to the literature on teens and libraries, particularly with technology as a focus. She has been a columnist for Tag Team Tech with *VOYA* and was elected YALSA president 2021–2022.

Marie L. Harris completed her Master of Library and Information Science at the University of North Carolina Greensboro in 2018. She began working for Charlotte Mecklenburg Library in Charlotte, North Carolina, in 2012 in the Loft at ImaginOn as a teen library services specialist. While in this role, she worked with Czarnecki to plan and conduct many technology-related programs for teens. The programs include facilitating the use of Studio i digital media lab for individuals and groups, planning and implementing a Google Maker Camp series for preteens and teens for two summers, collaborating with community experts to bring coding to the library, planning and implementing dozens of technology-related programs for the public, and partnering with a community teen robotics team. Harris is currently employed as a branch leader at the Davidson branch of the Charlotte Mecklenburg Library, where she manages a team of seven library staff members.

www.ingramcontent.com/pod-product-compliance
Lightning Source LLC
Chambersburg PA
CBHW082213300426
44117CB00016B/2796